Twayne's United States Authors Series

EDITOR OF THIS VOLUME

David J. Nordloh

Indiana University

Bill Nye

(Edgar Wilson Nye)

TUSAS 403

Bill Nye

BILL NYE

By DAVID B. KESTERSON
North Texas State University

TWAYNE PUBLISHERS
A DIVISION OF G. K. HALL & CO., BOSTON

Library of Congress Cataloging in Publication Data

Kesterson, David B   1938–
    Bill Nye.

(Twayne's United States authors series ; TUSAS 403)
        Bibliography: p. 159–65
            Includes index.
    1. Nye, Edgar Wilson, 1850–1896.   2.   Authors,
    American—19th century—Biography.
GK   √ PS2482.K38   818'.409   80-20971
            ISBN 0-8057-7332-0

To my parents, Homer and Dorothy Kesterson,
who lived in and loved Bill Nye's Laramie

"I will turn their mourning into joy,
and will comfort them
and make them rejoice from their sorrow"—

Jeremiah 31:13.

(Epitaph on Nye's tombstone in Calvary Episcopal churchyard,
Fletcher, N.C.)

Contents

About the Author

David Kesterson teaches courses in literature at North Texas State University, where he was recently designated Distinguished Alumni Professor. His specialty is American literature of the nineteenth century, especially American humor and Nathaniel Hawthorne. He has also taught at the University of Arkansas and North Carolina State University.

Dr. Kesterson was educated at Southwest Missouri State University and the University of Arkansas, where he was an NDEA Fellow. Active in a number of professional organizations, he has been president of the American Humor Studies Association. He co-founded and was first president of the Nathaniel Hawthorne Society; currently he edits the *Hawthorne Society Newsletter*. He also serves as associate editor of *Studies in the Novel* and the *Nathaniel Hawthorne Journal*.

Listed in the *Directory of American Scholars*, Professor Kesterson is the author of *Josh Billings* (Twayne, 1973) and *Bill Nye: The Western Writings* (1976); he has edited books of criticism on Mark Twain, Edgar Allan Poe, and Hawthorne's *The Marble Faun*. He has published articles on Hawthorne, Billings, Mark Twain, Cooper, Swift, and others in such journals as the *Nathaniel Hawthorne Journal*, *Illinois Quarterly*, *English Language Notes*, the *South Central Bulletin*, *Studies in American Humor*, the *Mark Twain Journal*, and *Notes on Modern American Literature*. He also reviews books for several major journals, among them *American Literature*. Currently he is writing a book on Nathaniel Hawthorne and has articles forthcoming on Hawthorne and Nye.

As a postscript, Dr. Kesterson mentions that he is an avid fan of early radio humor, which he views as a logical heir to the literary humor of the nineteenth century.

Preface

In the winter of 1978, United Press International released a syndicated feature on Edgar Wilson (Bill) Nye by Dan Chiszar. The title of the article varies, of course, from newspaper to newspaper, but the headlines usually proclaim Nye as a forgotten humorist. Indeed, according to the first sentence of the feature, "America, as it forgets most of its humorists, forgot Bill Nye."[1] For the most part, unfortunately, the article's assessment is correct. Bill Nye is hardly a household name, a fact that has caused me to utter countless repetitions of his name over the last few years when explaining to interested persons the subject of this book.

This Edgar Wilson Nye, however, actually rivaled Mark Twain for preeminence among America's literary comedians in the last half of the nineteenth century. He was the writer of whom Will M. Clemens wrote in 1882 that "during the past two years, [has] written a larger quantity and a better quality of first-class, genuine humor, than any other funny man in America,"[2] and who British literary critic Robert Ford said in 1897 "was a humourous writer of rare fertility, power, and variety, whose weekly contributions to periodical literature, were more extensively circulated and read than the pen-work of perhaps any other American author of this century; and he made, probably, the largest literary income of any journalist of his own time."[3] Nye was known from coast to coast, in England, and on the Continent as a witty, astute commentator on interests of the times and human nature in general. He was claimed by five widely divergent sections of this country: New England, because he was born in Maine; the Midwest, because he grew to maturity in Wisconsin; the far West, because he rose to fame in Laramie, Wyoming; New York, because he entered the world of big city newspapers and Broadway theater while living there; and the South, because he lived out his last—and highly productive—years in North Carolina. He was so well known that a letter to him from newspaper caricaturist Walter McDougall arrived safely on Nye's desk in New York when all that graced the envelope was McDougall's familiar comic drawing of the stick-figured, bulbous-headed comedian and the words "New York."[4]

The dual aims of this present study of Nye are to manifest the versatility of Nye as comic writer and lecturer and to reveal the nature of his humor, which is often complex. The former aspect of Nye's career is surprisingly expansive: he was an editor, writer of comic essays, sketches, and poems, lecturer, would-be novelist, author of burlesque histories, and playwright. His humor abounds in many techniques common to the works of the literary comedians in general (though it largely avoids the conscious misspellings and substandard grammar). Especially noteworthy is the abundance of humorous and satiric character sketches in Nye's works: he was fascinated with the human family and wrote about people more than any other subject. The West was important to Nye's humor, cutting deep, indelible marks into its mold. Nye had a propensity for turning the most serious situations (including his own chronic illness) into levity, but there is also a surprising dark, somewhat cynical vein in his humor, a strain that occasionally approaches the dark comedy of the middle to later twentieth century. Often reacting vehemently against sentimentalism and other excesses of romantic fiction, Nye was one of the critical realists who were partially responsible for ushering in the age of realism and naturalism.

This book deals with the full scope of Nye's career. To treat every newspaper column, essay, sketch, and poem that Nye wrote would be both impossible and undesirable, of course; thus, I have selected the ones that are most representative of his subjects and techniques or that give special flavor to his published books of collected short pieces. Nye as playwright and potential novelist I have discussed as best I can considering that none of the manuscripts or published versions are extant (in fact, the manuscript of his one novel, "Thelma," lies somewhere on the floor of the Atlantic as a result of shipwreck). Nye's original columns in the *Laramie* (Wyoming) *Boomerang*, the newspaper he named after his mule and which became famous, do not survive except as selected for his early books; thus I concentrate mainly on the published books during the Western phase of his career. Fortunately, complete files of the *New York World* and other newspapers for which he wrote as a syndicated columnist during the 1890s do exist, and thus I am able to cite them.

I find Nye an enjoyable writer on whom to work. True, there are the disconcerting blatant prejudices of which he was painfully guilty, but he wrote with a verve and enthusiasm, an exactness and penetration, a wit both amusing and poignant that make him far more appealing to the modern reader than most people are aware. Unfortunately, Nye has often been grouped categorically with the host of late nineteenth-century platform comedians, and the assumption is thus made that his humor was collective and derivative. Nothing could be further from the truth. He was among the last of those humorists to live and write, and his trenchant wit boasts an individualistic, sometimes complex tone that strikes surprisingly modern chords. That tone, plus Nye's universal exposure of sham and hypocrisy, impresses the contemporary reader with his relevance to modern times.

The plan of this book is both topical and chronological. Chapter 1 briefly surveys the major aspects of Nye's varied life and career. Chapter 2 focuses in detail on the Western phase of his development—an interlude that gave rise to his first significant writings. The third chapter breaks chronology and stops for a close look at the nature of Nye's humor. Nye as comic lecturer is the subject of chapter 4. His sojourn in Gotham, where he wrote for the *New York World* and matured as a writer, is covered in chapter 5. Chapter 6 explores his last years, when the mountains of North Carolina were his base of operation. The final chapter traces nearly a hundred years of critical reaction to Nye's humor and discusses whether that comedy is still funny and pertinent today.

In writing this book I am indebted, as my notes and references testify, to the pioneering scholarship of Walter Blair and T. A. Larson, preeminent among twentieth-century critics on Nye. The work of Nye's son, Frank Wilson Nye, has also proved extremely helpful. His book *Bill Nye: His Own Life Story* is the nearest approach to a biography-autobiography of Nye. For access to and permission to quote from their sizeable collection of published and unpublished materials on and about Nye, I am especially grateful to the American Heritage Center at the University of Wyoming, Gene M. Gressley, archivist.

For assistance and support of various kinds I am especially grateful to the Faculty Research Committee of North Texas State University, the library staff of North Texas State University—especially the willing, expert personnel of the Interlibrary Loan Office, the Humanities Division, and Special Collections—and English Department and Arts and Sciences administrators Chairman Sam H. Henderson and Dean Jim B. Pearson, all of whom know the debt I owe them.

A number of other libraries and special collections proved generous with their resources while I was gathering materials on and about Nye. These repositories include the Houghton Library at Harvard; the University of Wyoming Library; the Wyoming State Archives and Historical Department; the Albany County Library of Laramie, Wyoming;

the Laramie Plains Museum; the libraries of the University of Arizona, Southern Methodist University, Texas Christian University, Rice University, University of Oklahoma, University of Nebraska, University of California at Berkeley, University of Texas at Austin; Brown University, Bowdoin College, University of California at Los Angeles, University of Chicago, Columbia University, Dartmouth College, Haverford College, College of the Holy Cross, Indiana University, University of Michigan, Michigan State University, University of North Carolina at Chapel Hill, Princeton University, University of Virginia, Washington University, Yale University; the historical societies of Chicago, Missouri, Oregon, Pennsylvania, and Wisconsin; the Enoch Pratt Free Library, the Pack Memorial Library of Asheville, N.C., the Walter Hampden-Edwin Booth Theatre Collection and Library, the Library of Congress, the British Library, and the public libraries of New York (main library and performing arts branch at Lincoln Center), Chicago, Colorado Springs, Dallas, Los Angeles, and San Francisco. To the helpful curators of all these collections I am deeply indebted.

Among the individuals who have provided special assistance and encouragement are Emmett D. Chisum, David Crosson, and John Christopher of the University of Wyoming; Wayne Chatterton and James H. Maguire, coeditors of the Western Writers Series at Boise State University; Sylvia E. Bowman of Indiana University; James M. Linebarger of North Texas State University; Arthur Monke of Bowdoin College; John L. Idol, Jr., of Clemson University; Buford Jones of Duke University; Louis A. Rachow, editor of *Broadside*; Paul Meyers, curator of the Theater Collection at the New York Public Library at Lincoln Center; Thelma and the late Arlin Turner of Durham, N.C.; Richard and Priscilla Jewett of Asheville, N.C.; U.S. Representative Ray Roberts of Texas; Mrs. Alfred Chanutin of Middlebury, Vt.; Michael Winship, editor of the "Bibliography of American Literature" project at Harvard University; Dee Seadler of Silver Spring, Md.; Mr. James K. Polk of St. Augustine, Fl.; and two Nyes—James G. Nye, Jr., of Westborough, Mass., a descendant of Bill Nye, and Hermes Nye, Dallas attorney and author (no relation). I also wish to thank the editor of the *New York Times Book Review* Sunday supplement; my esteemed colleagues at North Texas State University, for their continued interest; and research assistants and typists Cathy Dollar, Sandra Gilbert, Karen Smith, and Sydney Beth King.

Above all, I am appreciative of the patience and support of my family and close friends, who continually gave of themselves in time and

Preface

indulgence while this book was being written. My parents, to whom this book is dedicated, were a virtual, willing guidebook to Bill Nye's Laramie. My wife Linda and sons Todd and Chad were understanding and helpful to a fault. Others too numerous to mention are aware of the debt I owe them. All the above individuals mentioned have helped make the writing of this book a pleasurable experience.

DAVID B. KESTERSON

North Texas State University

Chronology

1850   Edgar Wilson Nye born, 25 August, in Shirley, Maine, son of Franklin Nye, a Maine lumberman, and Elizabeth Mitchell Loring Nye.

?1852– Nye family lives in Hudson, Wisconsin. Nye attends local acad-
1876   emies for schooling; learns farming, teaches school, makes unsuccessful attempt to become attorney, writes for local newspapers.

1876   Leaves Wisconsin in spring for trek West, stopping in Wyoming where he becomes assistant editor of *Laramie Sentinel*. Assumes pen name "Bill" Nye. 7 November, elected justice of the peace. Becomes correspondent for *Denver Tribune* and *Cheyenne Sun*. Passes bar examination in fall; begins practice of law.

1877   7 March, marries Clara Frances (Fanny) Smith (his beloved "Catalpa"). 4 September, unsuccessful candidate for legislature of Territory of Wyoming. Appointed notary public early in year. Sometime between 1877 and 1880 becomes U.S. land commissioner. October, leaves employment of the *Sentinel*.

1880   November, reelected justice of peace.

1881   Helps found and becomes first editor of *Laramie Boomerang*, a daily and weekly newspaper named after Nye's mule. First issue in March. First book, *Bill Nye and Boomerang; or, The Tale of a Meek-Eyed Mule*.

1882   October, appointed U.S. postmaster in Laramie. *Forty Liars, and Other Lies*. November, is stricken with cerebrospinal meningitis.

1883   Convalesces in Greeley, Colorado, in winter and spring. Closes out affairs in Laramie during summer and fall, resigning from *Boomerang* and postmastership. October, moves back to Hudson, Wisconsin.

1884   *Baled Hay: A Drier Book Than Walt Whitman's "Leaves o' Grass."*

1885   In spring has first experience on stage as comic lecturer.

1886   First platform performance with James Whitcomb Riley.

Writes a play, *The Village Postmaster* (later rewritten as *The Cadi*).

1887   Moves to New York City and begins career as weekly humorous columnist for *New York World*. Lives in Tompkinsville on Staten Island. Lectures in New England, publishes *Remarks*. 28–29 November, Nye and Riley participate individually at important International Copyright League Benefit performance at New York's Chickering Hall.

1888   Nye-Riley lecturing partnership, advertised as "Twins of Genius," officially begins, opening in fall under management of James B. Pond. Nye and Riley publish *Nye and Riley's Railway Guide*. *Bill Nye's Chestnuts Old and New: Latest Gathering*, and *Bill Nye's Thinks*.

1889   June, Nye to Paris to cover international exposition for *New York World*. Visits London.

1890   January, Nye and Riley's last joint lecture, Nye finishing season with musical group as support. 1 July, son Ned dies. *An Almanac for 1891 by Bill Nye*. Writes concluding chapter for *His Fleeting Ideal: A Romance of Baffled Hypnotism*, a composite novel.

1891   March, moves from Long Island to Asheville, N.C., area, Nye having arranged with *World* to continue his column. June, drops weekly "letter" to *World* and soon goes with syndication under American Press Humorists Association. *The Cadi* runs for 125 performances on Broadway. Lectures with Alfred P. Burbank.

1892   Completes Buck Shoals, his rural abode at Arden, N.C., seat of his life and writings for his remaining four years.

1893   September, second trip abroad, to England. 28 September, a guest at dinner for Emile Zola. Late summer, attends and writes up World's Fair in Chicago.

1894   Lectures with William Hawley Smith, Burbank being terminally ill. *Bill Nye's History of the United States*. Resides in Washington, D.C. during winter to observe workings of government.

1895   January, sails for Bahamas; shipwrecks near Nassau. *The Stag Party* written with Paul M. Potter and produced on Broadway in December.

1896   Nye's precarious health fails. Dies 22 February at age forty-five. Buried 25 February in Calvary Episcopal churchyard. *Bill Nye's History of England from the Druids to the Reign of Henry VIII.*

1897 Posthumous publication of last book Nye prepared for publication, *A Guest at the Ludlow and Other Stories.*

CHAPTER 1

Life and Career

EDGAR Wilson Nye began his literary rise to fame as a small-town newspaperman in Wyoming in the late 1870s. Soon he was editing his own paper and writing weekly columns of witty commentary and anecdotes that gained local, regional, and then national attention. When he began to publish books of his popular writings and launched his career as a comic platform lecturer, his fame spread even faster and farther, making the name "Bill Nye" a household term throughout America and much of the Western world.

I Beginnings

"My biography is very brief and of little interest to the public. I was born August 25, 1850, in Shirley, Me., and moved West at the age of three years. I was expelled from Yale College in the summer of 1870 for refusing to divide a watermelon with the faculty."[1] Thus wrote Edgar Wilson (Bill) Nye to his newspaper public in 1894. The biographical squib is characteristic of Nye's writings in general—partially fact (dates and birthplace are correct), at least half fiction (he was two when he moved, and he never got near matriculating at Yale), and humorous and facetious overall.

Nye was born a Down Easter in Shirley, Maine, on 25 August 1850. His parents, both of English stock, were Franklin Nye, a Maine lumberman, and Elizabeth Mitchell Loring Nye, an intelligent, well-read, humorous woman who was a member of the prominent Loring family of Piscataquis County.[2] Nye was the oldest of three sons who lived to maturity, the younger brothers being Frank Mellen and Carroll Anderson Nye.[3] Young Nye was not to taste much of the flavor of New England, for his family left there when he was only two. But he later wrote of his hometown, after visiting it as an adult: " . . . my birthplace is all right as a birthplace. It was a good, quiet place in which to be born. All the old neighbors said that Shirley was a very quiet place up

19

to the time I was born there, and when I took my parents by the hand and gently led them away in the spring of '53, saying, 'Parents, this is no place for us,' it again became quiet."[4] And speaking of the family home in Shirley, he sentimentalized facetiously,

> Many memories now cluster about that old home. . . . There is, also, other bric-a-brac which has accumulated since I was born there. I took a small stone from the front yard as a kind of memento of the occasion and the place. I do not think it has been detected yet. There was another stone in the yard, so it may be weeks before any one finds out that I took one of them. (*RG*, 2)

When he took his parents "by the hand" and led them forth, it was to Hudson, Wisconsin, in the Kinnic Kinnic Valley of St. Croix County in the northwestern part of the state. This area of the county actually became the boyhood home of Bill Nye. Here he received his formal education—a nominal sixteen-week term at the local academy and two terms at a military school in nearby River Falls. At various stages during his young manhood in Wisconsin, Nye was a farmer (as his father had become since leaving Maine), miller, teacher, and student at law, though he was never able to pass the bar examination in Wisconsin. A law office in Chippewa Falls did employ him as a clerk, however.

It was also during these years in the Midwest that Nye developed his interest in writing—especially writing of a journalistic nature—and soon found success and satisfaction working as correspondent for two small locals, the *Hudson Star* and the *Chippewa Falls Weekly Herald*. Bolstered by his accomplishments on these two papers, he even contributed an article to the *Chicago Times*. Without realizing the implications for his future, Nye in Hudson experimented with and found success in two areas that would later be mainstays of his professional career: writing and public speaking. Apropos of the latter, Nye as a boy delighted in histrionics, especially enjoying performing before his family; he occasionally dressed up in a toga and performed Mark Antony's funeral oration or Spartacus' speech to the Romans.[5] In fact, there always remained in Nye something of the frustrated playactor. (His interest in the stage and his own attempts at writing for the theater are discussed below.)

Nye liked Wisconsin. In later life he enjoyed visiting the scene of his youth, once writing of it, "Here I am in the great Northwest, where I grew up as a lad and where my early life ran quiet as the clear brook by which I sported."[6] Fondly describing Hudson as "a handsome little city on the shores of Lake St. Croix,"[7] he recalled, with a tinge of local color, that

it was at Hudson that we used to bet on the date when navigation would open in the spring. There were no railroads then. When the first boat whistled in the spring people left their businesses, and sometimes broke off in the midst of an eloquent prayer—full of statistics and timely gossip and mere mention, news summary, baseball news and household hints—in order to run down to the landing and see the first boat come in.[8]

Hudson was a pleasant, if somewhat provincial, place in which to grow to maturity.

II *Enter "Bill" Nye of Laramie*

Wanderlust coupled with failure to find positions on Minneapolis and St. Paul newspapers prompted Nye to leave the Midwest in the spring of 1876. Now twenty-six years old and feeling confident that he would find some form of comfortable living on his own, Nye decided to travel westward until his funds were exhausted. Later, looking back on his move and reflecting on Horace Greeley's "Go West" axiom, Nye advised young people to travel extensively and learn firsthand the many areas of America. He would have the Northerner familiar with the South, the Down Easter with the West. Travel, he decided, provided the broadest education possible, and he concluded that instead of saying "Young man, go West," the better exhortation is "Young man, find out more about the country you live in."[9]

At Cheyenne, Territory of Wyoming, Nye's funds ran short, and he sought help in his job hunting from former Wisconsin attorney John J. Jenkins, then U.S. attorney for the Territory of Wyoming. Jenkins knew of a newspaper position open in nearby Laramie City and arranged with editor J. H. Hayford for Nye to be employed on the paper, the *Sentinel.* Nye now had his foot in the door in the town that he was soon to make famous and would be associated with in many ways for the rest of his life. Laramie City, located in the southeastern corner of Wyoming, was a boom town of 2,500 people, a railroad and a mining center. The mining aspect attracted Nye almost as much as the journalistic opportunities there, for he—like his later friend Mark

Twain—contracted mining fever and did his share of speculating on silver claims.

Nye's star rose rapidly in Laramie City. In a matter of months, after arriving in 1876, he was city editor of the *Sentinel*. He picked up his pen name "Bill" Nye while on the *Sentinel*, for though none of the readers knew an Edgar Wilson Nye, many were familiar with the impetuous, wily card shark Bill Nye of Bret Harte's poem "Plain Language From Truthful James," and thus the name stuck. Ironically, like the whole Western environment that Nye felt took matters into its own hands, often using human beings as pawns, even Nye's name was chosen for him, not by him.[10]

Nye spent only seven years in Laramie, but that period—1876 to 1883—was the busiest and probably the most exciting and fulfilling of his life. He worked for the *Sentinel* from 1876 to late 1877, was admitted to the Wyoming bar, and served as notary public, justice of the peace, United States land commissioner, and Laramie postmaster. He even ran, though unsuccessfully, for the territorial legislature. All this time his main line of work, however, was writing. He contributed to numerous magazines and newspapers (see chapter two), though he was most involved with the *Laramie Boomerang*, of which he was first editor. The *Boomerang*, established as a daily, soon expanded to include a companion weekly edition. Beginning with the issue of 11 March 1881 Nye contributed a humorous column almost daily, and for the weekly he gleaned from his writings a whole page of wit and humor. His style and approach were infectious, and circulation of the *Boomerang* rose skyward. By its second year, Nye's writings were being read nationally. Even Charles Dana of the *New York Sun* subscribed to the daily *Boomerang*.[11]

Nye's Laramie days were full in other respects. Family life became a favorite pastime after he married Clara Francis Smith of Illinois on 7 March 1877 and, while still in Laramie, became the proud father of two daughters (the five Nye sons, one of whom died in infancy, were born after the Nyes left the West). Nye's wife, called Fanny or Catalpa, was a congenial, charity-minded woman, and one who was quite talented and well trained in voice and piano.[12] Nye also published his first two books while living in Laramie City, *Bill Nye and Boomerang* (1881) and *Forty Liars and Other Lies* (1882); began preparing his third, *Baled Hay* (1884); and presided over the loosely structured "Forty Liars Club," a circle of hometown wits who convened to swap stories and just chat.

The halcyon days in Laramie were not to last long, however, as the year 1882 mounted a double attack of financial and management troubles with the *Boomerang* (see chapter 2) and serious illness to Nye in the form of cerebrospinal meningitis, a devastating disease which forced him to leave Laramie for lower elevations. Typical of Nye, however, is the good humor found in his facetious letter of 1 October 1883, in which he resigned his position as Laramie's postmaster. Addressed to the president of the United States, the open letter, "A Resign," is a perfect example of Nye's droll tomfoolery:

TO THE PRESIDENT OF THE UNITED STATES:

SIR.—I beg leave at this time to officially tender my resignation as postmaster at this place, and in due form to deliver the great seal and the key to the front door of the office. The safe combination is set on the numbers 33, 66, and 99, though I do not remember at this moment which comes first, or how many times you revolve the knob, or which direction you should turn it at first in order to make it operate.

There is some mining stock in my private drawer in the safe, which I have not yet removed. This stock you may have, if you desire it. It is a luxury, but you may have it. I have decided to keep a horse instead of this mining stock. The horse may not be so pretty, but it will cost less to keep him.

You will find the postal cards that have not been used under the distributing table, and the coal down in the cellar. If the stove draws too hard, close the damper in the pipe and shut the general delivery window. . . .

I need not say that I herewith transmit my resignation with great sorrow and genuine regret. We have toiled on together month after month, asking for no reward except the innate consciousness of rectitude and the salary as fixed by law. Now we are to separate. Here the roads seem to fork, as it were, and you and I, and the cabinet, must leave each other at this point. . . .

Mr. President, as an official of this Government I now retire. My term of office would not expire until 1886. I must, therefore, beg pardon for my eccentricity in resigning. It will be best, perhaps, to keep the heart-breaking news from the ears of European powers until the dangers of a financial panic are fully past. Then hurl it broadcast with a sickening thud.[13]

III   *Nye on the Boards*

After a brief stay of convalescence in Greeley, Colorado, in the winter and spring of 1883, the Nyes moved back to Hudson, Wisconsin. Nye, now thirty-three, was never again to enjoy good health after the attack of meningitis. But after the Laramie years his fame was assured, he was pleased to be back with former friends, and he enjoyed his rural retreat, dubbed "Slipperyelmhurst."[14] His third book, *Baled Hay*, appeared in 1884, and, when much of his former strength had been regained, he began lecturing in tandem with his Hoosier friend, the poet James Whitcomb Riley. Their combined presentations took the lecture circuit by storm. Their appeal, as Walter Blair has pointed out, was electric: "With little Riley serving as foil for the tall nonsensical Nye, the two entertained thousands in scores of cities and hamlets and reaped large returns for the [J. B.] Pond Lyceum Bureau. Capacity crowds greeted them everywhere. . . ."[15] The team of "Jamsie and Bill" flourished as a joint enterprise until 1890, when Riley's alcoholism caused him to sever the professional part of their relationship. Nye then signed other partners and continued touring the United States and Canada until near the time of his death in early 1896. He became one of the most popular comic lecturers ever, rivaling if not equaling the appeal of Mark Twain and Josh Billings. Although Nye enjoyed appearing on the platform, however, the strain of travel and performing undoubtedly led to his early death.

IV   *The* World *Calls*

Despite the years of lecturing, Nye remained a prolific writer. He published *Remarks* in 1887 and *Thinks* in 1888. And at the height of their joint lecture venture in 1888, he and Riley brought out their popular *Nye and Riley's Railway Guide*, a book containing the best of Riley's folksy verse and Nye's witty prose pieces.

While wintering in Asheville, North Carolina, in 1886, Nye sent the *New York World* a humorous sketch entitled "In My Sunny Southern Home," actually a spoof on the idea of a warm South in wintertime. *World* management liked the piece so well they made Nye a job offer he could not refuse, and the Nyes moved to New York early in 1887, Nye assuming his duties of writing a weekly humorous column for the Sunday *World*. After a few months of residence at New Brighton, the Nyes moved to Staten Island and settled in what Nye termed their "Schloss" at Tomkinsville. His position on the *World* required considerable travel. On behalf of the paper he scouted political and social goings-on in Washington, D.C., covered the Paris Exposition in 1889, and reported on London life. His relationship with the *World* ended temporarily, however, in June 1891 with a change of management at the newspaper, but his weekly column was transferred to other papers and syndicated widely in some seventy newspapers throughout the country.[16] The latest thoughts and antics of Bill Nye provided one of the most stimulating and enjoyable experiences in newspaper reading down through the last column that appeared on 23 February 1896, the day after his death.

V His "Sunny Southern Home": The Last Years

While he found his New York life stimulating and educational, Nye's precarious state of health called for a more temperate, year-round climate. Thus he moved his family to his favorite retreat, the Asheville, North Carolina, area, early in 1891, while still fully employed by the *World*. Concerning his beautiful one-hundred-acre farm at Arden, adjoining the vast Biltmore manor of George W. Vanderbilt, Nye wrote jestingly, "My farm is situated in Buncombe County, N.C. It is an oblique farm, with a fender on the lower edge to keep the potatoes from falling into George Vanderbilt's farm, which is below mine on the French Broad River."[17]

During these last six years of his life, Nye continued to pen his syndicated weekly "letter," as he called it, for Sunday newspapers, traveled as extensively as ever as a comic lecturer, and tried his hand at being a gentleman farmer in the North Carolina hills. New literary challenges greeted him during these years too, however. He wrote one play, *The Cadi*, for the Broadway stage in 1891, an autobiographical production which, to Nye's great satisfaction, ran for 125 engagements; and he collaborated with Paul Meredith Potter on another, though less successful, play—*The Stag Party*, a musical burlesque, in 1895. His books of this period included a volume of essays and sketches, *A Guest at the Ludlow* (posthumously published in 1897), and two volumes of extended burlesque: *Bill Nye's History of the United States* (1894) and the unfinished *Bill Nye's History of England from the Druids to the Reign of Henry VIII* (1896—also posthumous). He also wrote, in the vein of Josh Billings, a comic *Almanac for 1891*. For his newspaper publishers he made another European trip in 1893 and took a nearly disastrous excursion to the Bahamas in January of 1895, his ship wrecking and sinking. Nye survived, but the manuscript of his only novel, entitled "Thelma," did not.

As the new year 1896 began, Nye was obviously declining rapidly in health. The sporadic aftereffects of his cerebrospinal meningitis

became more persistent and his eyesight began to fail (bringing an end
to his lecturing), these symptoms climaxing in a stroke suffered in February. He died at his North Carolina home, Buck Shoals, on Washington's birthday and was buried in the Calvary Episcopal churchyard at
nearby Fletcher on 23 February 1896. Newspapers throughout the
United States, Canada, and England solemnly spoke of the passing of
a tradition. And, indeed, with the likes of Artemus Ward, Josh Billings,
and Petroleum Nasby all dead—and only a few humorists such as
Mark Twain and Finley P. Dunne remaining—it did appear that a
major American comic tradition was moribund. Editorial tributes to
Nye abounded in American newspapers, and friend James Whitcomb
Riley wrote the following memorial sonnet to his friend:

EDGAR WILSON NYE
February 22, 1896
The saddest silence falls when Laughter lays
    Finger on lip, and falteringly breaks
The glad voice into dying minor shakes
And quavers, lorn as airs the wind-harp plays
At urge of drearest Winter's bleakest days:
    A troubled hush, in which all hope forsakes
    Us, and the yearning upstrained vision aches
With tears that drown e'en heaven from our gaze.
Such silence—after such glad merriment!
    O prince of halest humor, wit and cheer!
    Could you yet speak to us, I doubt not we
Should catch your voice, still blithely eloquent
    Above all murmurings of sorrow here,
    Calling your love back to us laughingly.[18]

VI   *The Man and His World*

From accounts of Nye's contemporaries, the famous humorist seems
to have been gregarious and jocular by nature. He was the obvious
choice of leader for the fun-loving Forty Liars Club in Laramie. Laramie friend W. E. Chaplin remembered, "Socially Nye was a genial
companion and excellent company. He enjoyed good-fellowship. His
associates were the best men in town."[19] Nye's basic sense of humor
sustained him during the years of sporadic illness. An anonymous
editorial writer, eulogizing Nye on the weekend of his death, pointed
out that while Nye lay sick in bed with great pain, he "wrote that

which made others laugh with happiness. . . . [He] gibed merrily at misfortune and grasping a pen [made] jests while adversity was knocking at the door."[20] This was the merrier side of Nye that drew people to him and caused him to be in demand by small circles of friends and large lecture audiences alike. He was called a genial humorist, a gentle humorist; and indeed he was both at times.

Yet in no way was Nye's nature or his life simple and ingenuous. True, Nye seemed fairly contented with much of life, and he could even be nostalgic when looking back on boyhood homes and past experiences. But he was a complex man, his apparent genial nature concealing a driving ambition and a surprisingly somber view of life. He was desirous of success and fame and was willing to sacrifice greatly to attain them—even jeopardizing his own health. He scrutinized the world with a keen eye and sometimes lashed out at it with cutting satire. These more serious and complex components of Nye's character offset the image so often portrayed by his contemporaries of the wholly sanguine, easygoing Victorian gentleman.

Nye's interests, as we shall see in later chapters, were varied and far reaching. He was very much in the mainstream of events that filled his times. He wrote about Western mining, outlaws, boom towns, and hostile Indians; he discussed current developments in the arts, especially in drama and poetry; he probed complex agricultural problems and defended the American farmer against encroaching governmental controls; he commented on religion and marriage; he presented a modernist view of female suffrage and women's rights in general; he was politically concerned and often spoke out on behalf of Republican party ideals. In short, there is hardly a topic of his time that Nye did not touch on in his lectures, books, and newspaper columns (especially the last). He was certainly a classic humorist in the sense that much of his commentary and philosophy is timeless; but he was also a man absorbed in the world about him, and his writings manifest his heavy involvement.

Nye moved among some of the nineteenth century's most famous people: Mark Twain, Eugene Field, James Whitcomb Riley, Josh Billings, Bret Harte, to name only a few. He was no sycophant, however; he was just as pleased to find himself in the company of the Forty Liars Club—enjoying the folksy fellowship of Bill Root, Buck and Charles Bramel, Charles and Henry Wagner (all members of the stove-side circle in Laramie)—as to hobnob with the luminaries. He felt a strong rapport with the farmers in his area of North Carolina, for example.

But Nye could also be caustic and critical toward people. His hatred of artificiality and pretension, of hypocrisy and dishonesty, of license and degeneracy enlivens not a few of his essays, his scathing attacks on Oscar Wilde serving as some of the most poignant examples. Governmental officials and rival newspaper editors also frequently caught a drubbing from Nye, an aggressive mode of attack that he seemed to develop while living in the yet untamed West.

To most late nineteenth-century Americans, Bill Nye was the tall, angular, bald-headed comic figure portrayed by illustrator Walter McDougall in the Sunday *World*—the lean face adorned with a quizzical or deadpan expression. It did not take perceptive readers long, however, to realize that behind that bland look and apparently obsequious demeanor was a keen observer of human nature and an extremely trenchant humorist, one who viewed and recorded life in all its wonderful and bitter ironies, its triumphs and defeats.

CHAPTER 2

Early Writings: The Western Years

T HE Edgar Wilson Nye who arrived in Laramie City, Wyoming from Wisconsin in the spring of 1876 described himself as "a young man with pale seldom hair, and a broad open brow that bulged out into space like a sore thumb. He was slender in form like a parallel of longitude, with a nose on him that looked like a thing of life."[1] As was mentioned in chapter 1, this singular figure, during his seven years in Laramie City, served as postmaster, justice of the peace, United States land commissioner, notary public, and lawyer, and he tried unsuccessfully for the legislature. Above all, however, he was editor, journalist, and author, founding one of America's most famous small-town dailies and weeklies, and producing the materials for four books.

These Laramie years were the most formative of all on Nye's career as a humorist and journalist. Though he undoubtedly would have been a humorist had he never gone West, his humor would have taken a different tack had he remained an Easterner or Midwesterner. His life in the West had a marked effect on his attitude toward and approach to humor as well as on the subjects and types of humor he explored and used. There is no doubt that the seven short years Nye lived in Wyoming were the years that both christened "Bill" Nye and shaped Edgar Wilson Nye.[2]

I Booming the Boomerang

Nye's rise to national fame while in Laramie City was as a news-paper man—specifically as a humorous columnist for the *Laramie Boomerang*, which he helped found and named after his mule.

Beginning in May 1876 Nye first worked for the Laramie daily *Sentinel* as reporter and city editor under editor J. H. Hayford, who paid Nye twelve dollars a week and provided him room and board.[3] Though Nye did not have the constitution to be a topflight journalist—"he was unable to grasp details and any local account written by him was likely to be woefully deficient in essential points of interest, such for instance, as the amount of insurance or the loss to the property in accounts of disastrous fires"[4]—he successfully introduced humor into his columns from the very first. W. E. Chaplin, at the time typesetter for the *Sentinel*, wrote,

In his city work Nye's humor began to unfold. In all that he wrote there was a vein running from the sublime to the ridiculous and his rapid change from one to the other was the underlying power that made his sketches popular with the American people. The most commonplace item was given a turn that made the reader smile and there was laughter all through the local columns of the Sentinel [*sic*], a paper that had been as wise as an owl and as sober as a judge.[5]

While writing for the *Sentinel*, Nye also contributed columns to the *Denver Tribune*, edited by O. H. Rothaker. Nye's offerings—featured on the editorial page and covering a variety of subjects from mining to Indians—began late in 1879 and ran every week to ten days until mid-October 1880.[6] The importance of his association with the *Tribune*, aside from his meeting and becoming a lifelong friend of Eugene Field, who became city editor in the early 1880s, was that through this metropolitan paper he found a wider audience and escaped the often confining local topics. Thus, his appeal as a national humorist grew.[7] Nye's essays for the *Tribune*, like their Laramie counterparts, bristled with humor of a Western flavor. Levette J. Davidson writes that "with a spirit characteristic of the West he exaggerated, showed no respect for tradition or conventionality, and gave the real names of the victims of his satire."[8] Partially because of his success on the *Tribune* Nye was also soon contributing articles to such publications as the *Cheyenne Sun*, the *Detroit Free Press*, *Texas Siftings*, *Puck*, and *Peck's Sun* during the late 1870s and early 1880s.[9]

Back in Laramie, Nye temporarily abandoned local journalism by leaving the *Sentinel* in the autumn of 1877 to pursue his legal and political interests. For over three years he lived on his earnings as correspondent for other newspapers and on his meager salary as justice of the peace (fifty dollars a month), attorney, and land commissioner. Then in early 1881 Nye and other Republicans founded the *Laramie Boomerang*, in response to the need for a Republican rejoinder to the Democratic daily *Times*, which was founded in 1879 after the Republican *Sentinel* became a weekly. Nye was selected as editor, with a salary of $150 dollars a month. He personally went to Chicago to purchase the presses and other equipment with $3,000 capital provided by the corporation; and he had full management of the paper, attending to all administrative duties and even keeping the books. As editor he was in full charge of the "voice"—the editorial policy and direction— of the paper, greeting his readers with the following prospectus stated in the first issue:

We will spare our readers the usual programme of what we intend to do hereafter as a moulder of public opinion. We do this partly because we haven't clearly outlined our course yet in our own mind, and partly because some one might keep a file of the paper and annoy us with it in the years to come.

In all political questions which may arise the Boomerang will be Republican. We also intend to give due credit for what we copy from exchanges.

We shall, in addition to the above, perform several startling tricks of square-toed integrity which will arouse the wonder and surprise of those who have known us in the past.

With many thanks to the host of patrons and friends who have contributed to the very pronounced success of this enterprise, and with the earnest hope that they will not be disappointed, we advance to the foot-lights and hesitate a moment until the thunders of applause have died away in the distance.[10]

Nye's most important role on the *Boomerang*, as far as literary posterity is concerned, was, of course, as columnist. He wrote a daily humorous column and then collected his best efforts for a whole page in the weekly issue which soon grew out of the daily. It was these columns that made and sustained the *Boomerang*. Will M. Clemens wrote in 1882 that Nye "has, during the past two years, written a larger quantity and a better quality of first-class, genuine humor, than any other funny man in America."[11]

For a small-town newspaper in a village of 2,500, the *Boomerang* enjoyed phenomenal success, although locally, to quote Nye's complaint, circulation was only "150 to 250, counting dead-heads" ("The Newspaper," *R*, 426). National circulation, especially of the weekly edition, grew substantially during the second year of publication.[12] Not only did subscriptions come in from all states and several foreign countries, but leading newspapers throughout the Western World set up exchanges. Ironically, the *Boomerang* remained a small-time operation financially and was housed wherever it could garner an inexpensive corner. Its most infamous quarters were above a livery stable, a location that prompted the jocular Nye to erect a sign which instructed patrons of the *Boomerang* office either to take the stairs at the back of the stable or "twist the tail of the iron-gray mule and take the elevator" ("The Newspaper," R, 425).

Even the high popularity of Nye's humorous writings, however, could not stave off financial troubles and squabbles in the local corporation that controlled the *Boomerang,* and those problems—compounded by bickering between Nye and the other part owners and Nye's debilitating bout with cerebrospinal meningitis in November of 1882—brought an end to his affiliation with the *Boomerang.* In the summer and fall of 1883, he closed out his business with the paper.[13]

II *Eye Shades and Printer's Ink*

Nye made numerous comments in his newspaper columns and published books on the profession of newspaper editing. Most of those remarks concern an editor's travail. If not fussing with a dim kerosene lamp to overcome improper lighting,[14] then he was agonizing over a contributor's piece so technical and tedious that Nye wishes someone would club the author ("Poisons and Their Anecdotes," *BH,* 264). An editor is frequently embarrassed by having to make amends for incorrect information appearing in the columns of his paper ("The Amende Honorable," *BH,* 60–64); he is under constant pressure to socialize, an activity that detains him from his editing and writing duties.[15] Moreover, he has to live with or conquer the fear of attack by angered constituents who single out editors for assault or abuse.[16]

As an editor Nye was involved in several personal affronts. His former employer, editor J. H. Hayford, grew tired of his protégé in part because of Nye's success with the rival *Boomerang,* and he alluded to Nye as a buffoon, a "'gaseous comet, with its blazing tail [shooting] athwart the journalistic horizon of Laramie.'"[17] The *Cheyenne Sun* pronounced Nye a "natural born liar," dubbing him "weird and pixycal," and charged that if ever telephone lines were erected between Laramie and Cheyenne, Nye would tear them down with the lies from his "lop-sided jaws at work in front of the transmitter" ("Oh, No!" *BH,* 219). *Laramie Daily* editor L. D. Pease publicly condemned Nye as "'the insignificant pup that is suffered to befoul the pages of the Boomerang.'"[18]

Nye was quick to attack and counterattack, however, sometimes drubbing his adversaries. He critized the *New York Tribune* for its roving editor practice whereby the editor merely wrote or wired in and dictated policy. Nye retorted sarcastically, "We often feel that if we could get away from the hot, close office of *The Boomerang*, and roam around over Scandahoovia and the Bosphorus, and mould the policy of *The Boomerang* by telegraph, . . . we would be far happier" ("A Snort of Agony," *BH*, 129–30). He was sarcastic toward the editor of a Texas paper who, in an impertinent letter to Nye, asked Nye for an exchange ("Food for Thought," *FL*, 183–85), though he recanted when he learned the "editor" was actually two young girls. And he excoriated a petty editor who took offense at Nye's using the title of his newspaper in a simile:

The [Slimtown] *Harmonica* is not a *simile*. On the contrary, it is a parabola. It is a base, inferior isosceles, and its editor is nothing but a cosmopolitan hypothenuse; and if he wants to take it up, we may be found at our office at any time between the hours of A.M. and P.M. We were wrong in speaking of the *Harmonica* as a comparison or a *simile*; but we want it distinctly understood that we know what the *Harmonica* and its editor are, and we are not afraid to say so, either. They are pre-Adamite, vicarious isotherms, and we think that it is time the people of the west were apprized of that fact too. ("A Journalistic Connection," *NB*, 179)

It is no wonder, considering all the struggles that beset Nye as editor, that he confesses, in a facetious piece called "The Fun of Being President," that an editor is only slightly less care-worn than the highest administrator in the land (*FL*, 90–91).

On the subject of journalism itself Nye could be more sanguine. Despite its hardships, Nye's enthusiasm for his adopted profession permeates much of what he wrote about it. He proudly articulated lofty goals for the journalism of the *Boomerang*: "Excellence is what we seek, not bulk. Write better things and less of them, and you will do better, and the public will be pleased to see the change. . . . [*The Boomerang*] aims at elegance of diction, high-toned logic and pink cambric sentiment, at a moderate price . . ." ("Color Blindness," *BH*, 163). He appraised the state of journalism in the United States as follows:

The past fifty years have done much for the newspaper and periodical readers of the United States. That period has been fruitful of great advancement and a great reduction in price, but these are not all. Fifty years and less have classified information so that science and sense are conveniently found, and humor and nonsense have their proper sphere. All branches are pretty full of lively and thoroughly competent writers, who take hold of their own special work even as the thorough, quick-eyed mechanic takes hold of his line of labor and acquits himself in a creditable manner. The various lines of journalism may appear to be crowded, but they are not. There may be too much vagabond journalism, but the road that is traveled by the legitimate laborer is not crowded. The clean, Caucasian journalist, as he climbs the hill, is not crowded very much. He can make out to elbow his way toward the front, if he tries very hard. There may be too much James Crow science, and too much editorial vandalism and gush, and too much of the journalism for revenue only. There may be too much ringworm humor also, but there is still a demand for the scientific work of the true student. There is still a good market for honest editorial opinion, reliable news and fearless and funny paragraph work and character sketches, as the song and dance men would say. ("Parental Advice," *R*, 438)

In other places Nye discusses the rationale behind the editorial "we" ("We," *R*, 389–90) and analyzes journalistic style.[19]

He was not averse to commenting on the unsavory side of his profession, though. He resented the constant pressures of deadlines ("Knights of the Pen," *R*, 117–19), undeserved embarrassment suffered by conscientious journalists when others of their calling write poorly,[20] the unpleasantness of associating with obnoxious, ambitious young journalists ("A Journalistic Tenderfoot," *R*, 162–64),[21] and having to live with the disconcerting thought of possible physical and mental discomfort or harm. On the latter point, Nye once wrote to Will Clemens, "The West is well known as the home of fearless and deadly journalism. It brings out all there is in a man and throws him upon his own resources. It also throws him down stairs if he is not constantly on his guard."[22] A half serious piece entitled "Scientific" reveals the violent death of a *Boomerang* reporter in the arctic whose recovered diary breaks off just as a hungry bear approaches (*BH*, 184–88).

In all, journalism is a demanding, lifetime course of study and one requiring proficiency in intellectual and physical skills. Nye's essay "Suggestions for a School of Journalism"[23] outlines the rigors of the fourth estate. Proclaiming that the journalist must "strive to please the masses" and "make his whole life a study of human nature and an earnest effort to serve the great reading world collectively and individually" (*NB*, 32), Nye outlines a lifetime curriculum:

Prerequisites
  Two years for meditation and prayer
  Five years for familiarization with English orthography

Three years for body building and athletic training ("I have found in my
own journalistic history more cause for regret over my neglect of this
branch than any other.")
Regular Curriculum
Ten years for learning typography perfectly
Five years for learning to read and correct proof properly
Fifteen years for the study of American politics and civil service
(followed by a medical course in how to treat contusions and bullet
wounds)
Ten years for study of law
Ten years for study of theology
Ten years for mastering miscellaneous skills from cutting wood to learning
horsemanship. (*NB*, 32–34)

Upon completing this curriculum at age ninety-five, the student "will
have lost that wild, reckless and impulsive style so common among
younger and less experienced journalists. He will emerge from the
school with a light heart and a knowledge-box loaded up to the muzzle
with the most useful information" (*NB*, 34).

Though obviously greatly exaggerated, the above regimen at least
represents Nye's idea of the immense span of training and knowledge
the proficient journalist should have. Nye later advocated professional
schools of journalism, making a speech on their behalf before the Wisconsin State Press Association in 1885 and extolling Cornell University's
move in that direction in one of his *New York World* columns.[24] Nye
stressed the growth and importance of the press in the United States
and how it had become arbiter and spokesman for citizens, and thus
he emphasized the need for well-trained professionals to fill journalistic
shoes ("The Newspaper," *R*, 421–27).[25] Nye believed that "every
means should be used to pull this profession out of the mire of dense
ignorance and place it on the high, dry soil which leads to genius and
consanguinity."[26] That office Nye, at least as far as genius is concerned, performed while a journalist in Laramie; and he would
develop more of the consanguinity later in New York and North Carolina, when freed from the editor's desk and able to concentrate more
fully on his columns.

III   *Author Nye*

Nye's writings, of course, found other outlets besides newspaper columns while he was in Laramie. Early books of sketches, essays, satires,

and verses appeared and won popularity. The first three volumes—*Bill Nye and Boomerang, Forty Liars*, and *Baled Hay*—sold over 100,000 copies each and enjoyed ten editions.[27] These books, representing the best of Nye's Western writings, are largely collections of material originally appearing in the *Laramie Sentinel* and *Boomerang*. Nye frequently made some modifications of the original columns, shortening, adding transitions, and rewriting some portions. Other pieces are brand new. In general, because of their original newspaper appearance, the individual pieces in his books are quite short, averaging two to four pages. They are usually informal in structure and relaxed in tone. The best of them are not wanting in art and design despite the haste in which most of them must have originally been written to meet newspaper deadlines. They are not the carefully measured, finely chiseled aphoristic essays of Josh Billings, but they still achieve a sense of unity and coherence, maintaining a rather strict adherence to a central subject or main point. Nye rarely rambles or digresses out of carelessness.

Bill Nye and Boomerang; or, The Tale of a Meek-Eyed Mule, and Some Other Literary Gems, named after Nye's mule, consists of 114 selections, largely prose sketches, essays, burlesques, and satires, with most of the selections relating to the West: Indians, mines and mining, and comments on the land, the weather, local customs and features, and other aspects of life in the West. Also included is some of Nye's original poetry (discussed in chapter 5). Perhaps most characteristic of Nye's verse is the opening selection of the book, "Apostrophe to an Orphan Mule," a highly formal poem stylistically with mock-epical traits. The first stanza reads,

> Oh! lonely, gentle, unobtrusive mule!
> Thou standest idly 'gainst the azure sky,
> And sweetly, sadly singeth like a hired man.
>   Who taught thee thus to warble
> In the noontide heat and wrestle with
> Thy deep, corroding grief and joyless woe?
> Who taught thy simple heart
>   Its pent-up, wildly-warring waste
> Of wanton woe to carol forth upon
>   The silent air?   (*NB*, 7)

The humorous dedication of the book is to this same mule, "whose bright smile haunts me still, and whose low, mellow notes are ever sounding in my ears, to whom I owe all that I am as a great man, and whose presence has inspired me ever and anon throughout the years that are gone" (*NB*, [i]). An accompanying "Apology," addressed to publishers Belford and Clarke, points to the rather hurried, uneven nature of the book—a "rectangular mass of soul"—but Nye is sure that "a feeling of blessed and childlike confidence and assurance—and some more things of that nature—will follow the publication of this work." He admonishes his publishers to sell it at a "moderate price," then quips, "It is really priceless in value, but put it within the reach of all, and then turn it loose without a word of warning" (*NB*, [ii]).

Nye's second book, *Forty Liars and Other Lies*, contains 119 selections, again most of them prose and most concerned with Western themes. The title is taken from the Forty Liars Club that Nye presided over in Laramie, the title page quoting Lord Byron's line, "Praised be all liars and all lies!" Two of the selections treat meetings of the Rocky Mountain Division of the Independent Order of Forty Liars, one to choose the "Most Noble Prevaricator of the Year" ("The Forty Liars," *FL*, 7–12), the other to hear grossly exaggerated committee reports ("The Forty Liars. The April Meeting," *FL*, 47–52). They are among Nye's funniest burlesque pieces.

In his half-serious "Overture," or preface to *Forty Liars*, Nye points to the unexpected success of his first book and comically claims this second one is "in response to a clamoring appeal on the part of the American people" (*FL*, [5]). That "clamoring appeal" was loud enough for Nye to go to press the same year with a second edition of *Forty Liars* expanded by seventeen new items. Nye makes two special claims for *Forty Liars* in his preface: its durability—

This book marks an era in the history of classical literature. The spelling may be eccentric in places; and the etymology, syntax and prosody may be erroneous and abnormally picturesque, but the emaciated statements contained in its pages will shine on through the coming years, long after the statistics compiled with so much care by my comrade in the great field of literature, the United States Entomologist, shall have disappeared in a shoreless sea of oblivion. (*FL*, [5])

And its place in "the world's great march toward universal frankness"—

Instead of waiting for the beautiful and accomplished reader to search out and nail the prevarications with documentary evidence, there is a tacit admission on the start by the author that some little trifling falsehoods may have crept into the work, owing to the hurry and rush of preparation, and the unavoidably superficial criticism prior to its publication. (*FL*, 6)

Finally, Nye hopes persons mentioned in the book by name will not take offense (Nye's pen is sometimes acrid), but if they do they can call at the publishing house in Chicago and "glut their demoniac vengeance on the artist who illustrated the former book" (*FL*, 6).

Forty Liars contains several full-page illustrations by Livingston Hopkins, noted late nineteenth-century American illustrator. *Nye and Boomerang*, by contrast, offered only small etchings by an anonymous artist—perhaps Nye himself.

Before Nye left Laramie City in 1883, he clipped and took with him pages from the *Boomerang* office files in order to have a core of materials for his third book, *Baled Hay: A Drier Book Than Walt Whitman's "Leaves o' Grass,"* which he produced the next year. Cleverly illustrated by the famous Fred Opper of *Puck* (except for two drawings by Nye himself on pp. 105, 116), the book is composed of 135 selections—again largely essays, sketches, and burlesque narratives, but introducing a new technique, the paragraph: a brief space filler which is usually a pun, joke, or witticism, or sometimes just an interesting tidbit of information. The title page facetiously advertises the book as by the author of "'Bill Nye and Boomerang,' 'Forty Liars and Other Lies,' 'Goose-Neck Smith,' 'How Came Your Eye Out, and Your Nose Not Skun?' Etc., Etc., Etc.," and quotes a line from the Mark Twain-Bret Harte play *Ah Sin*: "Heap cold day when Melican man no lite em blook."

Nye dedicated *Baled Hay* to his wife, who has "courteously and heroically laughed at my feeble jokes, even when she did not feel like it" (*BH*, [3]), and he introduces the book with a "Piazza to the Third Volume." In his introduction Nye claims "no excuse for this last book of trite and beautiful sayings," and it will undoubtedly "add one more to the series of books for which I am to blame" (*BH*, 5). But it will perhaps please railroad travelers, Nye suggests; he claims he often rides the roads just to be assured of his continuing popularity (*BH*, 5).

Nye boasts in his preface to *Baled Hay* that he has "taken great care to thoroughly eradicate anything that would have the appearance of poetry in this work, and there is not a thought or suggestion contained in it that would soil the most delicate fabric" (*BH*, 6). Neither claim is truthful, however. Finally, Nye warns the reader about reading the book incorrectly: "Do not read it all at once, however, in order to see whether he married the girl or not. Take a little at a time, and it will cure gloom on the '*similia similibus curanter*' principle. If you read it all at once, and it gives you the heaves, I am glad of it, and you deserve it. I will not bind myself to write the obituary of such people" (*BH*, 6).

Nye's books throughout the remainder of his career—even including the posthumously published *A Guest at the Ludlow* (1897)—continue to reflect somewhat the influence of the West on Nye. His last major book to be substantially molded by the years in Laramie, however, is *Remarks* (1887). Some twenty-two percent of the selections relate in some way to the West. A weightier book than the first three—almost twice as long due both to an increased number of selections (191) and the pieces being more fully developed—*Remarks* shows definite change in Nye as a writer after he left the West. Not only are the essays and sketches longer and more substantive—the paragraph space fillers of *Baled Hay* having disappeared—but they reveal how Nye's interests had broadened over the few years since Laramie. For the first time he begins discussing history and biography, much of it surprisingly serious; he begins to talk about the lecture circuit and discuss such various subjects as boxing and situations in foreign countries. T. A. Larson might have a point when he claims Nye's post-Laramie wit deteriorated,[28] but the depth and richness of the pieces in *Remarks* compensate for any lessening of pointed humor. Here we can see Nye as a more complete writer, turning out penetrating, well-rounded sketches, narratives, and essays. A narrative episode such as "Twombley's Tale" (*R*, 68–70), for example, with its wildly funny antics of a man fallen to the bottom of a mine shaft, can stand on its own with the best of Mark Twain's exaggerated Western pieces.

Remarks can be viewed as a transitional volume. It looks forward to the more learned, mature Nye of the *New York World* period (see chapter 5), while it preserves much of the spirit of Nye's Laramie writings. Copiously illustrated by J. H. Smith, the book underwent seven editions[29] and was reprinted under alternate titles of *Bill Nye's Remarks* and *Bill Nye's Red Book*.

The title page of *Remarks* contains lines from Bret Harte's "Plain Language From Truthful James" (or "Heathen Chinee") poem about the card shark Bill Nye:

Ah Sin was his name;
And I shall not deny,

In regard to the same,
What the name might imply:
But his smile it was pensive and childlike,
As I frequent remarked to Bill Nye.

The book proper is launched by a page of Nye's "Directions," stating that this fourth volume is, he hopes, his best book yet—one that contains "my better thoughts, thoughts that I had thought when I was feeling well" (*R*, [v]). Nye considers it his "greatest and best book. It is the one that will live for weeks after other books have passed away." Despite the tongue-in-cheek comments, the first part of what he says is largely true: Nye had produced an interesting, polished, varied collection of humorous and serious pieces in *Remarks*.

IV *Westering*

To say that much of Nye's writing during his early years—both in newspapers and the books just described—concerned the American West is to understate the case considerably. Remove the Western subjects and Nye's early works would suffer near emasculation. The West, with its rugged terrain, extreme weather, and dynamic groups of people (miners, Mormons, Indians, outlaws, etc.) sculpted the material of Nye's early works. To live in the West was necessarily to absorb the milieu or reject it, reminds Diane E. Heestand:

Above all Laramie required physical and mental ruggedness for survival. The wind, the snow, the mountains, the rain, and the dryness made Laramie subject to the whims of nature. It was all these elements of nature along with the characters and happenings in Laramie which triggered Nye's humor. Indians, miners, Mormons, hangings, and gold strikes were just some of the Laramie local color. Nye exaggerated to achieve humor, but Laramie by nature was an exaggeration of rugged climate and survival of the fittest.[30]

Nye reacted to the many aspects of Western life more and more realistically the longer he lived there. It can be argued that just living in the Wyoming Territory and experiencing the violent weather, disturbances caused by outlaws and Indian uprisings, the chaotic status of mining, the crudities of frontier politics, and the struggles of a young author, editor, and public servant in a small Western town stripped Nye of what little romanticism he might have had left when he arrived in Cheyenne in 1876.

The very terrain, climate, and agriculture at Laramie's high altitude are frequent subjects of Nye's writings. Part of his reaction was positive: he could not resist the awesome scenic qualities of the West. "A Rocky Mountain Sunset" (*NB*, 61–62) records his almost bombastic description of one of his favorite sights, while "Ring Mountain" (*FL*, 128–29) and "Riding Down a Mountain" (*BH*, 284–87) exude Nye's fascination with the exotic formations and dizzy heights of the mountains. In such pieces he stands in awe of Western landscape. The weather and deplorable state of agriculture were quite different matters, however, and Nye's criticisms are poignant. In "The Weather and Some Other Things" (*NB*, 81–84) he deplores having to put on and take off "my buffalo overcoat for meals all through dog days," and he yearns "for a land where a man can take off his ulster and overshoes while he delivers a Fourth of July oration, without flying into the face of Providence and dying of pneumonia" (*NB*, 81). In "Agriculture at an Altitude of 7500 Feet" (*NB*, 199–201) his delight over receiving his spring planting seeds through the mail is tempered by the realization that in Laramie "winter lingers in the lap of spring till after the Fourth of July" (*NB*, 199–200). Having tried the "hot-bed" process with his crops the preceding year, Nye will use it for an ice cream freezer this summer since, even with the hot-bed, "several days in midsummer . . . my cabbage plants had to get out of that hot-bed and run up and down the garden walk to keep their feet from freezing" (*NB*, 201).

Though later Nye became something of a naturalist by avocation in the Blue Ridge Mountains of North Carolina, he declared that communing with Western nature is not possible with comfort. In fact, he gave up trying, as he indicates in one of his antipastoral pieces:

Nature is all right in her place, but you don't want to get too familiar with her. The everlasting snow-capped mountains, lifting their sunlit summits to the sky, are a pretty good thing, but they look better about thirty-seven and a half miles distant than they do when they are in bed with you, because they have got such cold feet. The little dancing torrent as it canters along to the ocean and bathes the feet of the mountain, is a pretty good thing—in a blue covered book—but when you come to grasp the reality and see that same little streamlet waddle along over the corns and chilblains on the foot of the mountain, and hear it murmur all night so that you can't sleep, the murmuring gets tiresome, and you begin to murmur yourself after a while. ("Sleeping With a Rocky Mountain," *FL*, 288)

Nye could be disheartened over his adopted West, often wishing for more refinement and culture and law-abiding ways. He objected to the carrying of guns ("The Pistol," *FL*, 105–6; "The Immediate Revolver,"

BH, 205–6); he wanted Western audiences to behave better at theatrical performances ("Another Suggestion," *BH*, 230–31); he missed good music in the West ("A Wail," *NB*, 278–79). On the other hand, he was sometimes in sympathy with Western provincialism ("Letter From Paris," and "Recollections of the Opera," *NB*, 26–28, 36–39), and defended the area against Eastern effetism, arrogance, and exploitation, openly admiring what he detected as a strong undercurrent of honesty, genuineness, and industriousness in the West. Easterners who came West with exaggerated preconceptions about its wildness ("He Wanted Blood," *FL*, 291–92; "The Holy Terror," *R*, 329–31), or tried to defraud the local residents in some way ("We Are Getting Cynical," *BH*, 236–38), or acted superior and more knowledgeable than the local folk ("The Gentle Youth From Leadville," *NB*, 201–2) fell prey to Nye's voracious pen. A characteristic counterattack is Nye's response to the arrogant outsider who "goes West with two dollars and forty cents in his pocket without brains enough to soil the most delicate Cambric handkerchief, and tries to play himself for a savant with so much knowledge that he has to shed information all the time to keep his abnormal knowledge from hurting him" ("One Kind of Fool," *R*, 250).

In short, Nye—while sometimes critical—frequently came to the defense of the West, for he found there a practicality, ingenuity, and sense of fairness that he greatly admired. For example, though not in favor of violence, Nye extolls the Western custom of hanging as an effective deterrent to crime: the "purple and suffocated appearance of the hanged is a depressing sight" ("Hung By Request," *BH*, 253). He suggests that if the murderer of President Garfield were sent West he would be hanged immediately, not set loose as he was likely to be in the East. If the East had vigilance committees, Nye continues, Washington D.C.'s census "would look as though the Asiatic cholera swept over the land" ("A Suggestion," *FL*, 126). Nye felt simply that the West had found satisfactory solutions to its problems that the more urban, sophisticated East had not.

Nye would keep the West, despite its shortcomings, as simple and unsullied as possible. Summing up his feelings in the excellent essay "No More Frontier" (*R*, 466–67), Nye, like Fenimore Cooper in *The Prairie*, laments the destructive inroads of civilization, especially the railroad and all that comes with it: "The system of building railroads into the wilderness, and then allowing the wilderness to develop afterward, has knocked the essential joy out of the pioneer" (*R*, 466). Even the roads in the West, where once the hopeful pioneers trod, are now strewn "with empty beer bottles and peach cans . . ." (*R*, 466).

V "A Field Full of Folk"

Nye's major subject is people. He wrote in *Bill Nye and Boomerang,* "During my short but eventful life I have given a large portion of my time to studying human nature. Studying human nature and rustling for grub, as the Psalmist has it, have occupied my time ever since I arrived at man's estate" ("Some Overland Tourists," *NB*, 229). One could certainly study human nature in the West of the 1870s and 1880s. In his works Nye portrays specific individuals—editors, statesmen, local "characters" such as Woodtick Williams—and whole groups of people—Indians, Mormons, the women of the West, miners, outlaws, and Chinese. As critic Ethel L. Lindsey has observed, "Wyoming, during the eighties, offered the same general kind of picaresque groups of peoples as Washington Irving had caricatured in 1809 in *Knickerbocker's History of New York*. In the place of the Dutch trader, the negro, and the Puritans, Nye had the Mormon, the Chinaman, and the politicians; while both Irving and Nye had the Indian."[31] Nye depicts Western personages with the same trenchant wit and satire present in his handling of other subjects. He is colorful and lively; he is also, unfortunately, sometimes strongly prejudiced toward certain groups of people.

His irritation over Eastern attitudes toward the West encompasses one of his most abused targets, American Indians. Because of his firsthand view of Indian activity in the West and his living there at the time of the Custer massacre at Little Big Horn in 1876 and the Ute uprising of 1879, Nye developed a general distaste for native Americans. He resented Eastern sympathy for the Indian, Easterners being chosen as administrators of Indian affairs, and what he considered Eastern ignorance of the true nature of the Indian and his ways. Easterners might be impressively knowledgeable of codfish and clams, admits Nye, in "The Eternal Fitness of Things" (*NB*, 218–20),[32] but not of Indians. He deplores the publication in Eastern newspapers of sympathetic accounts of American Indians, and claims that no "wails" on their behalf are ever heard in the West ("The Annual Wail," *BH*, 101–3).

Nye himself was once mentioned to the secretary of the interior as a likely candidate for appointment as Indian agent, but Nye begged off on two grounds: needing the seclusion and time for concentration required by "the true poet," and fearing that if placed in close proximity to the Indian "I may lose my self-command and kill him" ("Some Reasons Why I Can't Be An Indian Agent," *NB*, 52). Some of the most egregious examples of Nye's occasional sick humor concern dead Indians. In "The Crow Indian and His Caws" (*NB*, 247–50), he concludes that a dead Indian forms "a pleasing picture" and fondly projects the image "of a broad-shouldered, well-formed brave as he lies with his nerveless hand across a large hole in the pit of his stomach" (*NB*, 249). Nye attacks not only individual warriors, especially the Sioux Sitting Bull and Ute leader Colorow—emphasizing their mean natures and pettiness and undermining their feelings of self-grandeur—but also whole tribes, especially the Utes, though the Sioux and Shoshone receive their portion of his rancor also.[33]

Most surprisingly and paradoxically, considering his almost categorical antipathy toward Indians, Nye is complimentary of their oratorical skills,[34] an admiration almost certainly prompted in part by Nye's own interest in platform oratory of any sort (see chapter 4). In fact, characteristic of his complex, often contradictory nature, he occasionally writes sympathetic or at least dispassionate essays about Indians! "The Aged Indian's Lament" (*NB*, 161–63), an account of the last, sad, noble words of a warrior facing death, is a strange and unsuccessful mixture of sarcasm and pathos. "Ute Statesmanship" (*FL*, 144–48) is a surprisingly serious, somewhat sympathetic speech by Colorow to the Utes about their removal to other lands to make room for the whites. Colorow points out that these grounds are the land of all their history and that sadness and loss of pride are the results of their having to vacate. Nye's own keen sense of history and of innate justice cannot help but direct a measure of understanding and sympathy toward the Indian in his dilemma. One of Nye's late pieces on the Indian, published in 1892, is a Chesterfieldian letter from a Pawnee to his son. The tone is one of empathy on Nye's part.[35]

Nye's overall attitude toward the Indians seems to have been shaped by his contact with the more unsettled tribes of the troubled West. In his essay "Fifteen Years Apart" (*R*, 343–44) he traces his change in attitude from a youthful, idealistic view of the native American to his present feeling of repulsion, a change brought about by firsthand familiarity with the treacherous ways of the Wyoming tribes. His youthful view is stated in the first paragraph of "Fifteen Years Apart":

The American Indian approximates nearer to what man should be—manly, physically perfect, grand in character, and true to the instincts of his conscience—than any other race of beings, civilized or uncivilized. Where do we hear such noble sentiments or meet with such examples of heroism and self-sacrifice as the history of the American Indian furnishes? Where shall we go to hear again such oratory as that of Black Hawk and Logan? Certainly the records of our so-called civilization do not furnish it, and the present century is devoid of it. (*R*, 343)

When those words were written years ago, Nye cautions,

I had not seen any Indians, but I had read much. My blood boiled when I thought of the wrongs which our race had meted out to the red man. It was at the time when my blood was just coming to a boil that I penned the above paragraph. Ten years later I had changed my views somewhat, relative to the Indian, and frankly wrote to the government of the change. (*R*, 343–44)

A second group of Western peoples, the Latter-Day Saints, failed to draw even a modicum of understanding from Nye, however. He disliked them vehemently. As trainloads of Mormons passed through Laramie on their way to Salt Lake City from the East, Nye would view the cars of immigrants with utter disgust. He dwelled on what he considered their unsavory habits and poor hygiene ("The Fragrant Mormon," *NB*, 35–36; "The Mormons," *FL*, 93–4; "About the Mormons," *FL*, 148–50); their practice of polygamy ("An Explanation," *FL*, 193–94; "They Have Curbed Their Woe," *BH*, 250–51; "Causes For Thanksgiving," *R*, 302–4); their concept of revelation ("The Revelation Racket in Utah," and "Are You a Mormon?" *BH*, 189–92, 258–60); and their politics and disruptive civil laws which sometimes necessitated new legislation to control them ("The Morbidly Matrimonial Mormon," *FL*, 214–17; "Votes in Utah," *BH*, 279–82; "Murry and the Mormons," *R*, 199–200). Nye, of course, was not alone in his comic criticism of the Mormon sect. Mark Twain and Artemus Ward both had their say on the group. But Nye's satire is scathing and devastating, often resorting to invective. T. A. Larson has said that whereas the Mormons usually found a poor press in Laramie, "their harshest critic was Bill Nye."[36]

The Chinese in Wyoming were also targeted for Nye's satire, but they fared far better than the Indians and Mormons. Chinese laborers were brought into Wyoming in 1870 when the Union Pacific Railroad decided to hire them to help build and maintain their roads. Mining, laundry, and other jobs soon opened up for them.[37] The Chinese were unpopular with most Laramie area people because they worked for lower wages than white laborers demanded. Historian Larson points to the Rock Spring Massacre of 1885, in which twenty-eight Chinese were killed and hundreds evicted from town,[38] as an index of public feeling.

Nye was usually either lightly critical of the Chinese or remained neutral to their plight ("Hong Lee's Grand Benefit at Leadville," *NB*, 116–17; "How a Chinaman Rides a Broncho," *FL*, 180–83). His satire, however, sometimes thinly disguises a feeling of genuine admiration for the industrious ways of the Chinese and their perseverance in a hostile social climate. Writes Nye, "There is a feeling now too prevalent among our American people that the Chinaman should be driven away, but I do not join in the popular cry because I enjoy him too much, and he soothes me and cheers me when all the earth seems filled with woe" ("William Nye and the Heathen Chinee," *NB*, 112).

Another group of Western characters very much in evidence were the outlaws. There was no way to ignore them, even if they were a dark stain on the local color of the area. These bad men of the West, in fact, held a certain fascination for Nye that is revealed in his sketches of even the worst offenders. He discusses and depicts, in his usual seriocomic vein, the James and Younger brothers,[39] Big-Nose George Parrott, one Dangerous Davis, and lesser, anonymous outlaws, all of whom wreaked havoc in the early West. In one satire, "Killing off the James Boys" (*NB*, 49–50), Nye recounts the too frequent reports of the brothers' deaths—demises which curiously seemed to occur all over the country and over the period of several years. For the future, Nye insists, "Let us ignore the death of every plug who claims to be a James' boy, unless he identifies himself" (*NB*, 50). In another satire he surmises why, when Jesse actually died, no autopsy was performed: "They knew his mother would feel wretched and gloomy when she saw her son with his vitals in one market basket, and his vertebrae in another ("His Aged Mother," *BH*, 315–16). Besides, due to the havoc the James boys had caused, the Pinkerton Detective Agency was involved with autopsies of its own men!

From the antics of Dangerous Davis who, at his wedding, controls the ceremony with the threat of his Smith & Wesson and slings his new bride over his saddle ("The Nuptials of Dangerous Davis," *NB*, 250–52) to the numerous abortive attempts to hang Big-Nose George, Nye captures satirically the color and danger of the outlaw brigands of the

West. Despite his light treatment of these offenders, he is ever mindful
of the actual destruction caused by them as well as by the vigilance
committees who seek them out. On the subject of the vigilantes, his
sketch "The Opium Habit" (*R*, 63–64) depicts a mistaken lynching
which results in the death of an innocent man, and "They Let Him
Stay" (*FL*, 258–61) shows the members of a vigilance committee
becoming so overly zealous that they arbitrarily choose one townsper-
son to make an example of as they begin to purge their town of "evil."
Nye's sketches seem to look forward to the more sustained, psycholog-
ical view of lynch law found in Walter Van Tilburg Clark's *The Ox-
Bow Incident* (1940). Nye suggests a gun ban as a solution to most of
the troubles with outlaws and trigger-happy citizen groups alike,
though he is never specific in recommending a way to carry out such
a measure:

There is no more need of carrying a revolver in Wyoming than there is of
carrying an upright piano in the coat tail pocket. Those who carry revolvers
generally die by the revolver, and he who agitates the six-shooter, by the six-
shooter shall his blood be shed. When a man carries a gun he does so because
he has said or done something for which he expects to be attacked, so it is
safe to say that when a man goes about our peaceful streets, loaded, he has
been doing some little trick or other, and has in advance prepared himself
for a Smith-&-Wesson matinee. The other class of men who suffer from the
revolver comprises the white-livered and effeminate parties who ought to be
arrested for wearing men's clothes, and who never shoot anybody except by
accident. Fortunately they sometimes shoot themselves, and then the fool-
killer puts his coat on and rests half an hour. We have been writing these
things and obituaries alternately for several years, and yet there is no falling
off in the mortality. For every man who is righteously slain, there are about
a million law-abiding men, women and children murdered. Eternity's par-
quette is filled with people who got there by the self-cocking revolver route.
("The Immediate Revolver," *BH*, 205–6)

Nye concludes, in a sardonic commentary on life, "A man works
twenty years to become known as a scholar, a newspaper man and a
gentleman, while the illiterate murderer springs into immediate notoriety in a day, and the widow of his victim cannot even get her life
insurance. These things are what make people misanthropic and tenacious of their belief in a hell" (*BH*, 206).[40]
   In southern Wyoming and northern Colorado mining of silver, gold,
copper, and coal was flourishing at the time Nye was in Laramie. He

succumbed to mining fever, buying shares and "talking" mining in several of his columns. It is quite natural, then, that miners constitute another category of Western people whom Nye wrote about with interest and wit. Miners, Nye found, were of all types, but he capitalized on the lazy and dishonest ones in his writings, for, of course, they made good copy. In "The Calamity Jane Consolidated" (*NB*, 273–74) Nye depicts miner O'Toole, a sloppy worker and excessive imbiber in food and drink, who, when digging, "insisted on pouring the dirt down the back of his neck and then climbing out of the shaft with it and undressing himself with a gentle repose of manner which indicated that he had perfect command of himself and knew that his time was going right on all the same" (*NB*, 274). The cunning of some miners is further exemplified by a Mr. Thompson, who secures a contract to run a tunnel into a mountain to test a vein. He tunnels only through the deep snow, closes it over, and draws his $2,000 by claiming he has indeed succeeded in tapping the vein ("A $2000 Tunnel," *FL* 185–90). In other essays on mining,[41] Nye satirizes mining terminology and procedures, and he occasionally discusses his own ventures and claims, including an account of the mine he named after his mule Boomerang and another on which he cleared only a five-cent profit. Nye met with the same limited success in the mining business as did his friend Mark Twain. But it was an amusing side-interest for him and one that brought him into contact with some of the most colorful people in the Rocky Mountains.

Of all the Western peoples, Nye was proudest of and least prejudiced toward its women. He was a champion of the resourceful, reliable women of the West and an enthusiastic advocate of female suffrage. In this regard, he stands in sharp contrast to fellow humorists Artemus Ward and Josh Billings, who deplored the women's rights movement. Nye tried to recruit capable, right-minded women for the West ("Women Wanted," *FL*, 297–300). He stated that the West had no room, however, for weak, dependent women who desired to come West merely to procure husbands. In an open letter he responds to the inquiry of one Rosalinde by advising her to stay in Michigan: "We do not desire to ransack Michigan for affectionate but sap-headed girls" ("Rosalinde," *R*, 379).[42] Nye admires feminine women, but ones who also have a skein of independence and the mettle to survive the roughness of Western life. In "The Gentle Power of Woman's Influence" (*NB*, 255–57) he openly admires a Cummins City woman who, her cabin poles having been stolen by prospectors, takes a gun to the mining camp and conducts a meeting, quietly threatening the men. The

poles are returned. Nye praises the "inherent strength of weakness
... which enables woman amid a throng of reckless men to command
their respect and obedience sometimes where main strength and awk-
wardness would not avail" (*NB*, 257).

In 1890 Wyoming became the first state in the Union to allow
female suffrage.[43] Nye was proud of that fact and, while not a "howler
for female suffrage" ("Petticoats at the Polls," *R*, 453), supported the
results. In "What Woman's Suffrage Has Done for Wyoming" (*NB*,
167–70), "Our Forefathers" (*R*, 103–5), and "Petticoats at the Polls"
(*R*, 453–55), Nye is generally laudatory of women at the polls, only
occasionally uttering a facetious remark. In fact, he admits, in what
must have been a rare confession for his day, that nationally "there are
millions of women, no doubt, who are better qualified to vote, and yet
cannot, than millions of alleged men who do vote" ("Petticoats at the
Polls," *R*, 454). His support of women voting continued in effect the
rest of his life. Several of his nationally syndicated columns of the late
1880s and 1890s defend suffrage and attack those who denounce it.[44]

Nye was glad to see women beginning to develop the freedom and
individuality that lead to satisfying marriages for both husband and
wife. He championed the institution of marriage. He wrote one essay
on the advantages of remaining married over seeking divorce,[45]
penned another on the disadvantages of a man's marrying for beauty,[46]
and above all extolled the new kind of marriage partner woman was
becoming in society: "a girl whom we call 'a good feller,' who is a
better comrade, a wiser partner, a sweeter counselor and a more level-
headed guide, philosopher and friend than the best man on top of
sod."[47] Nye's own wife, his beloved "Catalpa," was undoubtedly the
model for his view of wives. She had developed her own interests early
in life and retained and nurtured them in her marriage; nevertheless,
she also shared and promoted Nye's interests and ambitions.[48]

In short, Nye was ahead of his times in supporting the advancement
of women. True, he did wish to see some male strongholds kept intact
(especially men's smoking rooms),[49] but he believed a sounder, more
intelligent relationship between the sexes was possible and necessary.
In the West Nye found the matrix of that new relationship.

VI *"Sliding Down Lead Mountain"*

In a humorous sketch resembling Robert Frost's poem "Brown's
Descent," Nye hilariously depicts a miner who ventures on the steep,
slick side of Lead Mountain in North Park, Colorado, and returns "a

good deal quicker than he aimed to" ("Sliding Down Lead Mountain," *FL*, 66). As we have seen in chapter 1, Nye himself had to leave the mountains and the West unexpectedly because of the deleterious effects of high altitude on him after he contracted meningitis. In addition, his business relationships with the other *Laramie Boomerang* stockholders were becoming strained, if not perilous, and thus his departure was perhaps timely. His enemies notwithstanding, most of Nye's Western friends and acquaintances regretted his leaving as much as he himself was sorry to depart. His associates on the *Denver Tribune* sponsored a farewell dinner for him, with Eugene Field, O. H. Rothaker, and William Lightfoot Visscher making the arrangements.[50] Nye wrote a clever "A Resign" letter (quoted in chapter 1) and tried to be philosophical about his move. But the seven happy, successful years in Laramie were heavy on his mind, as his curious open letter entitled "A Word in Self-Defense" (*BH*, 81) attests:

> It might be well in closing to say a word in defense of myself.
>
> The varied and uniformly erroneous notions expressed recently as to my plans for the future, naturally call for some kind of an expression on this point over my own signature. In the first place, it devolves upon me to regain my health in full if it takes fourteen years. I shall not, therefore, "publish a book," "prepare an youmorous lecture," "visit Florida," "probate the estate of Lydia E. Pinkham, deceased," nor make any other grand break till I have once more the old vigor and elasticity, and gurgling laugh of other days.
>
> In the meantime, let it be remembered that my home is in Laramie City, and that unless the common council pass an ordinance against it, I shall return in July if I can make the trip between snow storms, and evade the peculiarities of a tardy and reluctant spring.
>
> > Bill Nye.[51]

Nye would continue to use the West in his writings in many different ways. His own experiences there as editor, author, and civil servant, plus his associations with and feelings about the peoples of the West, became an inextricable part of him. Years later, when he was a columnist for the *New York World* and seventy syndicated newspapers, he would continue to write of the West with a tone of excited nostalgia. He looked forward to his lecture tours in the West with unabashed anticipation and wrote them up with enthusiasm in his Sunday columns. Western subjects—horses, guns, traveling shows, mining fever, harsh weather, the status of the Chinese, Mormons, Indians, and women—fill the pages of Nye's Laramie books. Moreover, the Western years shaped and indelibly stamped Nye's humorous techniques, a subject to be discussed in the next chapter.

CHAPTER 3

The Cap and Bells: Nye's Humor

THUS far we have referred to Nye's humor only indirectly, mainly citing examples from his newspaper articles and early books to illustrate the subject matter of his writings. As our casual look becomes close analysis, we must remember that Nye's wit sought multiple outlets: magazines, comic journals, almanacs, burlesque histories, lectures, jest books, and railway readers (all to be discussed in later chapters), aside from the newspaper columns and usual books of essays and sketches. As Walter Blair reminds us, "When Nye began his career as a humorist, there were numerous ways in which he could win prominence, and he used practically all of them."[1]

I Borrowings

In his dissertation "The Background of Bill Nye in American Humor," the most thorough study of Nye's relationship to early American humorous writing, Walter Blair has said that in some ways Nye is a "typical" American humorist: "Nye was the last of a line of American humorists which sprang into being about 1830 [with Seba Smith's Jack Downing], humorists who depicted life around them in almost every part of the nation, and who . . . had many tricks and many attitudes in common. . . . They used varied methods of creating vivid pictures of the people and of the institutions of almost every section."[2]

Blair's dissertation catalogs forms and techniques of humor used by Nye, tracing their origins in early American humorists and usually commenting on how Nye does or does not follow suit with each particular form or technique. Blair's historical tracings can hardly be improved upon. But there is need to probe deeper into the distinctive humorous nature of Bill Nye, draw together his chief humorous traits, and examine his own comments on humor. For though he was perhaps in many ways a "typical" humorist in sharing some of the same subjects, forms, and techniques of humorists from Seba Smith to Mark Twain, still his was a unique voice, a humorous expression significantly

51

different from each of the other comic journalists-platform humorists
(who in turn, of course, had their own distinctive traits).

II   *Style and Techniques*

Nye's prose style is one of the most engaging aspects of his writing.
It is abundantly clear and promotes a sense of ease and spontaneity.
Directness and lack of adornment, except when he is burlesquing
inflated writing and grandiose subjects, reign supreme. The tone of his
essays is generally familiar, relaxed, and conversational, with lively
verbal irony constantly at play. Though his pieces are generally short,
he eschews epigrammatic style. Though concise, they lack the pithiness
of a Josh Billings.

Nye's sentences flow together, but often take surprising turns which
create humor. Edmund H. Eitel feels Nye's humor lies in "surprises,
in freaks of the imagination, not, as with [James Whitcomb] Riley, in
impersonations."[3] His incongruous comparisons—and Stephen Leacock has spoken of incongruity as the very basis of humor[4]—are a
major feature of his wit. Confirms W. E. Chaplin, "In all that he wrote
there was a vein running from the sublime to the ridiculous and his
rapid change from one to the other was the underlying power that
made his sketches popular with the American people."[5] Albert E. Hancock, addressing Nye's "keen intellectual perception," believes Nye
was "a genius at antithesis": "He had the sharp discriminating eye
which sees like one gifted with superior powers of vision. He perceived
the detail which fits an artistic purpose—the unexpected detail which
brings a trifle into bold relief, which subtly debases dignity, or which
sheds the flash-light of truth on a humbug."[6] Indeed, Nye's method of
treating his subjects is to probe and turn with felicity of phrase, leaving
little unexamined or unmined for humorous possibilities and allowing
nothing of pretense or dishonesty to pass unscathed.

One of Nye's chief successes in writing humor is his sense of comic
timing. He constantly surprises the reader with unexpected happenings
and reversals of character and situation, traits which, added to the
lively verbal irony, keep his humor sparkling. The suspense of the
episode "A Thrilling Experience" (*R*, 131–33), for example, is worked
out with deft timing. Nye retires to his hotel room after a lecture,
thinks he hears breathing in the room, eventually shoots in the dark,
and finally discovers the culprit is the steam radiator. Comic genius is
evident in the timing of "Twombley's Tale"(*R*, 68–70), an absurd burlesque in which G. O. P. Twombley relates his experience of falling

accidentally into a mine shaft. Just as the reader expects the narrator to expand one line of thought, he switches to another. While Twombley is pondering how to tell time in the bottom of the pit and has the reader absorbed in his problem of having no watch, a second person abruptly falls down the shaft—this time a woman. The absurd incidents and remarks continue to pile up, Nye's acute sense of comic timing and turn of phrase continuing to the very last anticlimactic line: "We [Twombley and his "fallen" woman companion] got out of the shaft and eloped" (*R*, 70).

Clever wording, picturesque speech, and special workings of sounds and puns follow closely upon the heels of timing and verbal irony as key techniques of Nye's. Sometimes he merely plays with sound effects, indulging in puns, excessive alliteration or assonance, and onomatopoeia. In "The Buckness Wherewith The Buck Beer Bucketh" (*NB*, 175–76) he facetiously concludes that "the buckness of the buck beer bucketh with a mighty buck" (*NB*, 176). Usually, however, Nye moves beyond mere punning into the area of picturesque speech and clever phraseology. In the bout with the steam radiator mentioned above, for example, he describes his shooting at the heater, while in bed reading a Smith & Wesson instruction book, as opening "the volume at the first chapter and [addressing] a thirty-eight calibre remark in the direction of the breath in the corner" (*R*, 132). Nye describes a culprit's hanging as his being "unanimously chosen by a convention of six property-holders of the county to jump from a new pine platform into the sweet subsequently" ("Patrick Oleson," *FL*, 75–80). The young man who goes out into the world timidly and inexperienced is "the young-man-afraid-of-the-sawbuck, the human being with the unlaundried spinal column." Afraid to ride horses, this person never experienced the thrill of being "yanked through the shimmering sunlight at the tail of a two-year-old" ("One Kind Of A Boy," *BH*, 29–32). In an essay on noses, Nye proclaims a wax nose attractive, "but in a warm room it is apt to get excited and wander down into the mustache, or it may stray away under the collar ..." ("Regarding the Nose," *BH*, 160). In "The Codfish" (*BH*, 313–14) Nye jests over the smell of the fish: "When he enters our household, we feel his all pervading presence, like the perfume of wood violets, or the seductive odor of a dead mouse in the piano" (*BH*, 314). He continues,

Friends may visit us and go away, to be forgotten with the advent of a new face; but the cold, calm, silent corpse of the codfish cannot be forgotten. Its chastened influence permeates the entire ranch. It steals into the parlor, like an unbidden guest, and flavors the costly curtains and the high-priced lam-brequins. It enters the dark closet and dallies lovingly with your swallow-tail coat. It goes into your sleeping apartment, and makes its home in your glove box and your handkerchief case. (*BH*, 314)

In short, whether he is describing a miner "Sliding Down A Mountain In A Gold Pan" (*FL*, 160–64), the platform collapsing in the midst of his Fourth of July speech ("Drawbacks Of Public Life," *NB*, 64–65), or being "thrown into immediate juxtaposition" with the bumble-bee ("The Temperature Of The Bumble-Bee," *NB*, 63), the language sparkles with picturesque phrases. Nye even uses the device of the "rhapsody," a technique discussed by Louis Hasley.[7] The device consists of highly exaggerated, eloquent speech that contrasts sharply with Nye's actual feelings about what he is describing, the tension between form and thought providing humor. He will wax so poetic about a Western sunset, for example, that there is little doubt about his description being spurious: "The golden bars of resplendent light are shot across the deep blue of heaven, the fleecy clouds are tipped and bordered with pale gold, while the heavy billows of bronze are floating in a mighty ocean of the softest azure" ("A Rocky Mountain Sunset," *NB*, 62).

One of the standard comic language techniques used by many of the literary comedians—cacography, or intentional misspelling for comic effect—is rarely practiced by Nye, however. He felt that misspellings and poor grammar were the dated devices of Artemus Ward, Bill Arp, Petroleum Nasby, and Josh Billings. He occasionally uses these devices in a mock letter written to him by some semiliterate corresponding author, and he employs them effectively to achieve homey, rural flavor in the "Dear Henry" letters of 1883 and following—letters from an old fashioned farmer to his modernist son.[8] Otherwise, fortunately, he largely avoids misspellings and intentional faulty grammar.

Nor did he have much use for the techniques of proverbialism and antiproverbialism, mainly because his style was not generally epigram-matic. Only occasionally are there lists of aphorisms in the Josh Billings vein, and even then they fail to achieve the verbal economy of a Billings maxim.[9]

The stock devices of understatement and anticlimax, however, pervade Nye's writings and form a major part of his verbal wit and irony. His skill with the former is evident in his sketch "Mania For Marking Clothes" (*BH*, 154–58). After his friend has put three shots through the narrator's valise containing clothing—in order to mark the clothing for future identification—the narrator remarks, "After that a coolness sprang up between us, and the warm friendship that had existed so long was more or less busted" (*BH*, 154). Anticlimax reigns in "A Hairbreadth Escape" (*NB*, 74–76) in which Nye recalls accidentally losing a mole to the fumbling hands of a barber: "I did not care very particularly for the mole, and did not need it particularly, but at the same time I had not decided to take it off at that time. In fact I had worn it so long that I had become attached to it. It had also become attached to me" (*NB*, 76). Further examples abound. In fact, the two techniques are so prevalent in Nye as to crop up in practically every humorous piece he wrote. He was a master of last lines—the usual place, of course, for understatement and anticlimax.

In the last chapter we examined the influence of the West on Nye's subject matter and realistic approach, concluding that the flavor of the West was partially responsible for the development of Nye's distinctive voice. The same can be said for some of his salient techniques—especially the various forms of exaggeration, of sick and violent humor, and of particular slants of satire and burlesque. As Levette J. Davidson has suggested, "With a spirit characteristic of the West he exaggerated, showed no respect for tradition or conventionality, and gave the real names of the victims of his satire."[10] It is conceivable, of course, that Nye would have used these techniques had he never ventured West; these modes, after all, were shared by humorists of the Down East and Old Southwestern schools too. But Nye's living in the West and facing some quite coarse, turbulent aspects of Western life undoubtedly affected his use of these devices, increasing their poignancy and the frequency with which they appear in his writings.

Exaggeration, of course, is an undisputed characteristic of frontier or Western humor. In Nye it usually takes the form of improbable incident, inflated language, and slapstick antic rather than the most common form of exaggeration in frontier humor, the tall tale. Walter Blair has already pointed out that the tall tale is not a major form of humor in Nye, citing only four or five examples in each of Nye's Western books.[11] The explanation lies in the fact that his anecdotes and sketches so often involve Nye himself that he refuses to follow the tall-tale tradition of ascribing the story to a fictional personage and thus creating a prevaricating character, such as Twain's Bemis in *Roughing It*.

Other types of exaggeration are plentiful, however, especially the absurdly improbable incident. In "Dirty Murphy" (*NB*, 60–61) a man uses dynamite to blast a hole in order to get to a frozen water pipe, and the explosion launches a wash tub clear into outer space and through the Milky Way. In another piece Nye thanks a contributor for the gift of an "indestructible pumpkin pie" so tough that "when Gabriel sounds the proclamation that time is no more, this blasted pie will stand up without a blush and say, 'Here, Gabriel, is where you get your nice, fresh pie, and don't you forget it, either'" ("Thanks," *NB*, 282). Already mentioned is the zany, exaggerated humor of the "Forty Liars" club meetings recorded in Nye's second book, but that volume also contains a good example of the exaggerated account in the essay on the sheep's anatomy, "A Word About Wild Sheep" (*NB*, 52–53). Obviously, Nye's exaggeration sometimes takes the form of slapstick. In "Drawbacks of Public Life" (*NB*, 64–65), while Nye is publicly reading the Declaration of Independence as his Fourth of July oration, the stage collapses, burying him under the chaplain, the featured orator of the day, and the Fourth Infantry Band, and all the while the greased pig is running between Nye's legs and continually knocking him down when he attempts to stand. In a classic line of understatement, Nye quips, "I never knew the reading of the Declaration of Independence to have such a telling effect" (*NB*, 65).

Closely akin to exaggeration is another form of humor clearly influenced by Nye's life in the West—the cruel, violent, dangerous episodes that are clearly intended to evoke humor, albeit of a dark or sick hue. As we know, life on the frontier and in the American West was often harsh, dangerous, and generally unpleasant. Frontier and Western humor such as Nye's sought relief from its stark realities by overindulging its excesses on the printed page. Nye's violent humorous pieces usually pertain to the treacherous Western landscape or weather, dangerous vocations such as mining or working on hazardous mountain railroads, or unruly human behavior. In "Yanked to Eternity" (*BH*, 225–57), a drunken section crew loses its brakes while speeding down a mountain in a work cart. One man is forced to leap off with a rope tied about him in order to stop the car and save the other men. The man is killed, of course, and shows up at the base of the mountain only "in part." Mischievous miners in "A Mining Experiment" (*BH*, 238) play a trick on a youth who claims to be a mining expert by telling him to drive a stick of dynamite into a hole with an axe. He is killed in the resulting explosion, and the men are said to be still trying to get him out of the ground "with ammonia and a tooth brush." A long, treacherous tunnel on the railroad to Gunnison, Colorado, is so narrow that if passengers happen to lean out the window, "the company [has to] hire an extra man to go through the tunnel twice a day and wipe the remains of tourists off the walls" ("A Letter From Leadville," *BH*, 271–72). In the sketch "Dessicated Mule" (*R*, 345–46) a "snub" cable drawing mules up one side of Pike's Peak by force of a counterweight on the other side draws too fast; the unfortunate mules "didn' touch the ground but once in three thousand feet, but they struck the canopy of heaven several times." What was left of the "dessicated" mules was "fractional" (*R*, 346).

Though not a dominant trait, sick or dark humor shows up occasionally throughout Nye's career. The stark and depressing realities of the West are one source, but there is also an undeniable trace of the sardonic and perverse in Nye's nature that likewise accounts for the less appealing humor. Already quoted in chapter 2 is Nye's gruesome praise of a dead Indian ("The Crow Indian And His Caws," *NB*, 247–50). His syndicated newspaper column for 24 September 1893, describing his experiences at the Chicago World's Fair, contains these callous lines:

Day before yesterday I had a glass of beer, and the band seemed to play a little bit better than it had before since I have been on the grounds.

A man also came near falling off the big Ferris wheel 300 feet to the ground, and in every way it was the pleasantest I have yet saw whilst there.[12]

Nye's humor, obviously, could be far from kind and gentle.

III   *Satires and Burlesques*

It goes without saying that satire is a major part of Bill Nye's writings. However, satire is an extremely broad term when applied to his works. In the first place, it is both a method, or technique, and also a literary form. Second, the range of satiric tones and subjects in Nye's writing is expansive, varying from light mockery of current events, institutions, and manners, to vicious invective hurled at individuals; it also includes literary burlesques and parodies. Though Nye could get personal in his attacks, usually his topics were, as Davidson has said, general hypocrisy, affectation, and dishonesty.[13] Educator John Dewey reportedly felt that "Bill Nye was a great satirist. Few Americans have done more to expose pretense and superstition."[14]

Nye's personal attacks could be as defamatory as those of Juvenal and Jonathan Swift. Rival editors, politicians, and anyone exhibiting arrogance, deceit, shallowness, or crass ignorance fell under Nye's rapier. As W. E. Chaplin points out, Nye "could meet unkind words with flashing, vitriolic sarcasm."[15] Thus when the editor of the *Sweetwater Gazette* engaged Nye in controversy, Nye counterattacked in his *Boomerang* editorial: "We have nothing more to say to the editor of the *Sweetwater Gazette*. Aside from the fact that he is a squint-eyed, consumptive liar, with a breath like a buzzard and a record like a convict, we don't know anything against him" ("Our Compliments," *FL*, 94). Politicians, especially Democrats, could evoke the worst of Nye's attacks. Henry Rothschild Crosby, candidate for the Wyoming Supreme Court, offended Nye and others with his cajolery and personal obnoxiousness. Nye actually drew an uncomplimentary caricature to accompany his character analysis of Crosby, explaining in the caption, "It isn't very pretty, but it is horribly accurate. It is so life-like, that it seems as though I could almost detect his maroon-colored breath" ("A Little Puff," *BH*, 116). In another column he viciously rebukes a naive, impetuous Vermonter who aspires to be a humorist[16] and elsewhere attacks an Englishman, Hamilton Aidé, who has visited America and then published a criticism of the country after reaching the safety of home. In one of the milder paragraphs, Nye writes, "I do not know Mr. Aidé very well, but it has been my misfortune to cross his plague stricken trail once or twice to gnaw at the closely cropped herbage among the hills where yet still lingered the echo of his bray."[17] Toward English writer Oscar Wilde, who made quite a stir when he visited America in 1882, Nye had only the most caustic and derogatory remarks to make, once attacking him in a scathing poem with such invective as "Thou blue-nosed clam/With pimply, bulging brow..." ("Apostrophe Addressed To O. Wilde," *FL*, 275).[18] Obviously, a main trait of Nye's invective is his naming his targets and thrusting at them directly; there are no MacFleknoes or Flimnaps in Nye's satires, no circuitous flanking movements. Such direct assault occasionally backfired on Nye, as might be supposed. T. A. Larson reports that on at least two occasions in Laramie Nye was forced into hiding because of comments he had made about local citizens.[19]

When out from under the mantle of invective, Nye's satire is often pleasant and amusing. He was adept at light burlesque. In fact, Walter Blair has commented that, with the exceptions of Charles H. Webb and Bret Harte, Nye made more use of burlesque than any other nineteenth-century humorist.[20] Nye particularly liked to burlesque or parody literary productions—especially sentimental or adventure fiction—oratory, and history. His burlesques of fiction serve here as excellent examples of his approach to his targets. He mocked not only the traditional stock elements of plot and characterization, but, with his realist's eye, also denigrated the romantic traits of sentimentality, bombast, and melodrama. Blair has pointed out that Nye's technique in burlesquing fiction is to "exaggerate the unlifelike characterizations, the absurd plots, and the water-color backgrounds which were fashionable, until their absurdity, thus magnified, became quite evident." What resulted, Blair continues, was that humorists such as Nye became "the best critics of contemporary popular fiction."[21]

The Western flavor is again often present in these fictional burlesques, as is evident by their titles: "Pumpkin Jim; Or The Tale Of A Busted Jackass Rabbit" (*NB*, 104–12) and "The Club-Footed Lover of Piute Pass: A Tale Of Love And Cold Pizen" (*NB*, 190–94). The former is an exaggerated melodrama about a cowboy who is practically incapacitated by falling off his horse; besides breaking a leg in three places, one of his ribs was pushed "through the liver and into the ground, thus pinning him to the earth and preventing him from rising" (*NB*, 105). In the latter, a rancher with the "*nom de corral*" of Henry Ward Beecher attempts to steal another man's lover, only to be poisoned and relieved of his favorite mule. Imagery and ornateness are strained to the limit, and comic understatement comes into play in Nye's lines, "The orb of day rode slowly down the crimson west. The snow-clad mountains stood leaning against the purple sky. They had done so on several occasions before" (*NB*, 92).

Occasional biblical parody shows up in Nye's burlesques. This technique, as well as a general flippant irreverence, is common in the works of the literary comedians, of course. Nye's "The Parable Of The Unjust Steward" (*NB*, 84–87) and "The Parable Of The Prodigal Son" (*NB*, 87–90) serve as examples. The humorous mixture of high style and pedestrian subject, coupled with comic incongruity, creates a successful burlesque:

Now there was a certain rich man in those days, who kept a large inn on the American plan. . . .
And the inn-keeper said unto himself, "Go to;" and he was very wroth, insomuch that he tore his beard and swore a large, dark-blue oath about the size of a man's hand. . . .

And behold one day the inn-keeper took a large tumble even unto himself, and also unto the racket of Keno-El-Pharo the son of Ahaz Ben Bunko. . . .

And Keno-El-Pharo abode long in the land over against St. Louis, and he was steward in one of the great inns for many years, and he wore good clothes day by day and waxed fat, and he rested his stomach on the counter, and he said to himself, ha! ha! ("The Parable Of The Unjust Steward," passim)

A final point about Nye's burlesques, especially those on literature, is that while they ostensibly attack certain traditions and institutions, actually they thinly veil Nye's own love of writing fiction and poetry, revealing something of a frustrated novelist and narrator in Nye. As we shall discuss further in chapters 5 and 6, throughout his career Nye tried his hand with varying success at several kinds, styles, and lengths of fiction and poetry. He had a hunger for writing narrative that becomes increasingly evident in his later newspaper columns and books. He even attempted a novel in the 1890s, and many of his sketches are first-person monologues or character descriptions of real or imaginary people, leading Walter Blair to observe that "Nye used character portrayal much more frequently than any of his contemporaries."[22] Thus, though the burlesque narratives were written as honest satires on the one hand, on the other they gave Nye cause to try his hand at writing narration, a form he probably would have carried much farther had his whole orientation and situation as a journalist been different.

IV   *The Humorist on Humor*

"I am endeavoring in my own poor way to make folly appear foolish and to make men better by speaking disrespectfully of their errors," E. H. Eitel quotes Nye as saying concerning his purpose as a humorist.[23] Nye set himself up as first target, feeling that to laugh at oneself is the initial step toward fulfilling the role of humorist and satirist. Recalling, in an article written in 1893, an embarrassing childhood incident in which he finally decided to laugh at himself, Nye concludes, "Since then I have turned my personal sorrows into the enjoyment of others till it is my philosophy that we may turn our misfortunes into groceries, give outrageous fortune the laugh and mix things with her, as our athletic society says."[24] He thought it great fun when, upon visiting a wax works museum and standing at mute attention while he watched a sculptor mold the figure of Columbus, he himself was mistaken by onlookers for a new wax figure.[25] The Chaucerian technique of turning the humor on himself is consistent throughout Nye's newspaper columns especially. It is a device that he used to put his readers at ease with him before he subtly enlarged the satirical frame to include them in the general follies of society.

Frequently Nye discussed some specific facet of humor. Sometimes his topic was generic, as in "The Joke Pure and Simple,"[26] a facetious piece that examines the contributions of Demosthenes, Archimedes, Elijah, and others to the development of the joke proper. Or he would comment on the advantages and disadvantages of being a humorist, as in his witty dialogue "The Youmorist" (*BH*, 69–72). Whereas everyone expects the humorist to be lighthearted perpetually, the humorist is keenly aware of human sorrow and misery and is often not in a mood to be funny. Nye implies that being a humorist is a disease that can ruin one's life; one of the participants in the dialogue, in fact, admonishes parents not to let their children become humorists:

Whether your child be a son or daughter, it matters not. Discourage the first sign of approaching humor. It is easier to bust the backbone of the first little, tender jokelet that sticks its head through the virgin soil, than it is to allow the slimy folds of your son's youmorous lecture to be wrapped about you, and to bring your gray hairs with sorrow to the grave. (*BH*, 72)

At other times Nye's subject is American humor in general, or American humor compared to and contrasted with that of another nationality, especially England. As early as the Wyoming years, Nye meditated on the characteristics of American humor, detecting a major fault in its "coarseness and lack of polish" ("Portuguese Without A Master," *NB*, 172). When compared to the polish and international flavor of Portuguese humor, which Nye had supposedly been studying along with Portuguese grammar, American humor comes up wanting: "Americans may for years to come be able to furnish a good, fair, stoga joke that will do to stub around home with, but they cannot design a joke that will do to dress up in and wear on great occasions. . . . We may command the smoking car and Congress trade, but Portugal must furnish the easy riding, gentle, picnic and croquet joke." (*NB*, 173). In "The Approaching Humorist" (*R*, 260–61) Nye teasingly replies to a conceited, would-be humorist that there is certainly a lamentable "dearth of humor in America" at the moment and he has wondered, until he received this man's letter, just who the "coming humorist" was to be. He advises Herman, the aspiring humorist, to learn spelling and grammar first, however, though he admits—with a nod to the practices of other literary comedians—that that step is not absolutely necessary: "A friend of mine named Billings has done well as a humorist, though his knowledge of spelling seems to be pitiably deficient. Grammar is convenient where a humorist desires to put on style or show off before crowned heads, but it is not absolutely indispensable" (R, 260).

Probably Nye spends more time contrasting American and British humor than discussing any other aspect of the subject. Early in his career he described the elusiveness of British humor versus the more direct, utilitarian nature of American humor: "The humor of England, if closely examined, will be found just about ready to drop over the picket fence into the arena, but never quite making connections" ("English Humor," BH, 299). In a later essay discussing the quiet subtlety of British humor, Nye finds it

very soothing to me. Compared with the peppery wit of the French and the insidious, surprising and stimulating humor of our own country, English humor reminds me of boiled rice. Boiled rice taken in moderation isn't going to hurt any man. It furnishes an excuse for the gestures of eating and rounds out the abdomen to a degree—to several degrees, in fact—yet it does not excite one.

It is so with English humor. I have known men to apply themselves to English humor for several years and thin out their blood that way so that they prolonged their lives for a long time.[27]

The Punch and Judy show, Nye writes condescendingly in another column,

is a kind of humor that appeals to the English, and yet it leaves the brain tissue unimpaired. It is a broad yet pure humor, which is prompt in its action on the English mind, producing no dangerous relapse or secondary symptoms. Some kinds of humor are highly injurious to the British, because they may recur to the mind at a future time, when the victim is not prepared, or, still worse, the point of the joke may break out suddenly on a future generation and create much trouble. You might spring a subtle piece of humor on an Englishman and produce no appreciable effect, but think of his helpless grandchild on whom the humorous heritage might fall.[28]

The Briton's inability to grasp American humor, despite (or perhaps because of) its audaciousness, is the topic of a column in which Nye vents his frustrations over trying to engage an English friend in repartee. Nye concludes that it is a "national calamity" that England does not appreciate America's brand of wit:

When I said that some of our most serious wars had been with members of the Bull family, notably with John and Sitting, he seemed stunned.

"I beg pardon," said he, which means that he did not understand me. . . .

Afterward, I learned that if I wished to say anything facetious I had to prepare his mental soil for it by two or three roars of laughter. Then by planting the joke in a warm place, with a sunny exposure and fertilizing it with a jab or two in his ribs, the bonmot could eventually sprout. It is a national calamity.[29]

Perhaps more than reflecting a cultural breach between the two countries, Nye's English friend simply was not prepared for the barrage of constant wit from a man who, as Eugene Debs pointed out, saw "a humorous side to everything" with his "keen and searching eye." "Humor was to him the essence of wisdom, the savor of life. He delighted in expressing himself and interpreting his friends in terms of kindly, genial, good-natured humor."[30]

In sum, the essence of Bill Nye's humor lies in his ability to dress up commonplace phenomena and observations in colorful vestments of incongruity. A. E. Hancock carries the metaphor further, stating that the man who dresses facts in the "habiliments of convention" is a "mere scribe"; if that scribe adds "intellectual interpretation of causes and consequences," he becomes a "philosophic historian." But finally—and this step is apt for Nye—"if, with a sharp eye for the incongruous, he wilfully brings his facts into unnatural and unexpected relations, he produces that distortion which is one of the fundamental qualities of humor. The mere scribe thus becomes a jester with the cap and bells."[31] Nye was that gifted jester.

CHAPTER 4

Nye As Comic Lecturer

W HEN in October of 1883 the thirty-three-year-old Nye left Laramie City for good and moved back to Hudson, Wisconsin, the future appeared anything but bright for him. True, there was a measure of excitement in returning to the scene of his youthful days; but Nye was still less than hearty due to the meningitis, and there were doubts about how much activity his system would be able to withstand in the future. When he left Laramie, however, he had with him three advantages that would tide him over through his illness and make possible future opportunities: an indomitable spirit that would always rise above personal misfortune and adversity, material for his third book, *Baled Hay*, and a firmly established fame that would bring the world to his doorstep. It so happened that one supplicant to appear at that doorstep was the famous Major James B. Pond, lecture entrepreneur *par excellence*. He had wanted Nye to be one of his platform regulars since Laramie days. Nye now consented and added an entirely new dimension to his career, one that was to bring much wealth, even more renown, and a great measure of satisfaction, as Nye would become one of the premier comic lecturers, crisscrossing the United States and Canada from 1886 to 1896. But his very success on the platform would also help hasten his early death at the age of forty-five, because of the strenuous demands the lecture circuit would make on his already disease-weakened constitution.

I A Lifetime Interest

From boyhood onward Nye was fascinated by the art of public speaking of any sort: formal oratory, afterdinner speaking, and—of course—eventually comic lecturing. His aunt Mary Loring Woodworth recalled that on rainy days in the Hudson, Wisconsin, home the boy Nye would costume himself in a makeshift toga and entertain the family by delivering "Mark Antony's address or Spartacus with variations."[1]

64

In his books and newspaper columns, Nye frequently addressed the subject of oratory, reacting to it at times both seriously and comically. We saw in chapter 2 that Indian oratory was one of the few aspects of the native Americans that Nye revered and took seriously. He also discussed, surveyed, or emulated classical oratory in such pieces as "All About Oratory" (*R*, 356–58), "Speech of Spartacus" (*NB*, 126–30),[2] and "Day Of The Spell-binder Is Past, Says Nye."[3] In the Spartacus oration, Nye depicts the Roman warrior exhorting his band of gladiators to escape their enslavement and die free rather than "having our shin bones polished off by Numidian lions, amid the groans and hisses of a snide Roman populace" (*NB*, 130). The speech is serious, direct, and actually quite effective in its careful construction and resulting emotional impact. In the "Day of the Spell-binder" article, Nye discusses the oratorical tradition of Cicero and Demosthenes and Indian oratory (claiming the Indian is an orator by nature), and defends comic lecturing from the charge that the platform humorists have ruined oratory. The main reason oratory has died, posits Nye, is that "we live in a most practical and prosaic time. When a city can be destroyed at a distance of eight miles and a large iron cook stove full of explosives may be thrown into New York from beyond Fire Island, what sort of employment is there for a poet laureate or a big-browed orator with a cloven breath?"[4]

Before he ever mounted the platform professionally, Nye was delivering Fourth of July speeches in Laramie, as we have seen, and he continued to speak before clubs, societies, and at commencements the rest of his life.[5] In *Kings of the Platform and Pulpit*, Melville D. Landon quotes verbatim Nye's clever speech to a photographers' convention in New York, in which Nye cleverly and philosophically depicted the seven stages of man's life as they would appear if photographed.[6]

Although he was fond of the art, Nye did not hold lecturing so sacred that it escaped his usual satirical eye. A spoof on Socrates' failure as an orator becomes a clever commentary on the difficulty lecturers have sustaining audience allegiance.[7] The Fourth of July orations by both Nye himself and Indian orators often turn into burlesque, as does the one examined in chapter 3 where the platform collapses with Nye.[8] Political speeches are parodied in "The Ute Presidential Convention" (*NB*, 183–89), and the Sunday school exordium is mimicked in "Skowhegan Onderdonk On The Plan of Salvation" (*FL*, 32–33). Walter Blair's survey of the historical background of oratorical burlesque concludes that "the oratorical style between 1830 and 1896, particularly vicious, was a natural target for humorous men,"[9] and Blair points to predecessors of Nye who frequently burlesqued it: Seba Smith, James Russell Lowell, Joseph G. Baldwin, Johnson Jones Hooper, George W. Harris, Robert K. Newell, Artemus Ward, and David Ross Locke. Nye's contemporaries Max Adeler and Robert Burdette also used orations as humorous material, Blair recalls.[10] Nye's parody of oratory is similar to that of the other practitioners. Blair elaborates: "With the grand style he mingled homely words and phrases, and for the picture book version of contemporary conditions he substituted the realists' knowledge of facts. And he ended the speech, not with a hair-raising peroration, but with an absurd anti-climax."[11]

Thus, from serious to comic view, Nye was always interested in oratory and public speaking of any sort. The stage held a fascination for him that even led to theatrical and play-writing aspirations, a subject explored in chapter 6. His knowledge of the history of comic lecturing was anything but superficial. Nye's propensity for history carried over into the background of this field too. Just as he wrote a survey of classical oratory in the above mentioned "All About Oratory," he seriously probed the origins of comic lecturing in a newspaper article entitled "From The Greenroom."[12] Reviewing the history of both the theater and comic lecturing, Nye links the two by saying Artemus Ward (viewed by Nye as the "pioneer American humorist") received his inspiration from popular American stage actor Joseph Jefferson:

Charlie Browne (Artemus Ward) had amused his friends many times by his look of intense sadness even while he was in some grotesque situation which itself made everybody laugh, but he did not know that he was acting. He did not know that he was doing a comedy part without support on stage till he saw Jefferson in "A Terrible Fix."

Then his Yankee shrewdness showed him that he might utilize this power to his own advantage and the entertainment of others. . . .

So he became the first lecturer in America and England who could please and delight an audience alone with his humor, heightened by the art of the stage.[13]

Indeed, from standpoints of both lifetime interest and scholarly knowledge of his subject, Nye was prepared for the role of stage lecturer as few others were.

II *Background*

Nye's great interest in oratory and the stage notwithstanding, it was quite natural for a well-known personality—especially a writer—to turn to platform lecturing in the nineteenth century, for lecturing and public programs constituted one of the richest cultural traditions of the times. As means of enlightenment, moral instruction, and entertainment, lecturing had flourished in America since the early 1830s when the American Lyceum was established.[14] Lecture halls—ubiquitous in the East and West by 1850—drew crowds to hear the likes of eloquent Ralph Waldo Emerson and Henry Ward Beecher and, by the 1860s, the dry-witted comedians Artemus Ward, Josh Billings, and others. Nye and Mark Twain were among the last of the popular platform funny men.

With so many speakers traveling throughout the United States and Canada, a need for simplification of scheduling and an opportunity to make money off circuits gave rise to the lecture managers who would employ the lecturer, plan his annual itinerary (guaranteeing him a set number of engagements for the season), and in return take a percentage of the profits as managerial fee. Such were two titans of the lecturing business, managers James Clark Redpath and Major James B. Pond. Redpath in 1869 launched his Boston Lyceum Bureau and soon was sponsoring such "$100-a-night-men" as Mark Twain, Josh Billings, and eventually Nye himself. Major Pond, first part of Redpath's office, later ran a similar operation out of New York.[15] These lecture managers were at once business managers, friends, and sometimes father confessors to their "stars." They pampered their lecturers, taking on all the endless, tiresome details of scheduling and making other arrangements such as handling publicity, setting up special engagements, and serving as banker. The star was thus left free to concentrate on performing, though, as we shall see in Nye's case, an endless profusion of woes could still turn the lecture circuit into a nightmare.

III   *Enter Nye*

Major Pond remembered that he first approached Nye about platform lecturing while the latter was still editing the *Laramie Boomerang*, thus prior to the fall of 1883. "I told him people were reading and talking of him all over the country, and that I believed he could make money lecturing."[16] But it was not until Nye returned to Hudson, overcame the immediate effects of his disease, and published *Baled Hay* that he gave serious thought to lecturing and tested his strength and ability with a trial lecture.

Two letters written in March 1885 reveal Nye's plans and initial success. He wrote to Major Pond on 9 March:

I have just returned from an experimental trip where I tried it on a service town. I remineseed [sic] for an hour in 15 or 20 minute doses and the audience fairly jarred the windows loose and made me promise to come back in May. The other hour was taken up by solos, and 4 tellers trios. It is not much hard work as I had been led to suppose. I enjoyed it as well as the audience did. Now if we can get Lulu Hurst or a Song and Dance artist to take up that other 60 minutes, it will be fun for us and exeurvating [sic] wealth in the high future. I do not underscore that word because I am not an Englishman.[17]

Almost as interesting as seeing Nye's format is sensing his naiveté when he discusses the ease of lecturing. Such early enthusiasm on the part of a novice would not continue long. The letter continues, "While you concoct a plot for next season, I can be practicing now and then, get on friendly terms with my liver and hang my swallow-tail coat over the clothesline a day or two." A week later Nye sent his plans to another acquaintance, spelling out how the musical interlude would mesh with his lecturing and pointing to his early successes:

Seriously however, I have an hour's reading prepared in three 20 minute doses and when I have been asked to come pending the negotiations with Miss Hurst, I have made the proposition to give my 60 minutes with local vocal and instrumental music to take up another hour alternating with me, for instance, two or three musical numbers and then like a clap of thunder from a clear sky comes the Prima Donna from the Rocky Mountains. In this way I can give my part of the show at Middletown for instance at $50. When next season in company with Miss Hurst or the Two-Headed Nightingale, it would be probably four times that sum. Where I have tried this so far it has been a great success and I have had to promise to go back again.[18]

Thus 1885 was Nye's preparatory year for the platform. From then on until the end of his life he was busily engaged in lecturing, his tours interrupted only by occasional personal and family illness and business trips for the *New York World* or the American Press Humorists Association (see chapters 5 and 6).

Nye's first official lecture under Major Pond's management took place early in 1886 in Bridgeport, Connecticut. The YMCA had asked for Nye at $150. The evening went well, the house being "the largest . . . they remembered having on an opening night."[19] But after the lecture Nye experienced one of the frequent harassments of the lecture circuit—reluctance on the part of the local committee to pay up and pay fully. Though Nye finally got his money, it was not pocketed without hard feelings having developed between the parties.

Nye had not worked long into his first season until he realized the frustration and fatigue that resulted from lecturing alone. A chief difficulty lay in sustaining a high peak of audience reaction throughout the whole performance. With the audience often limp and laughed out halfway through a program, the humorist "had to proceed to the end of the programme without a response," as Major Pond observed.[20] Besides, it was physically and mentally exhausting. Nye decided, therefore, to join in partnership and thus share the evening's speaking parts. He confided to Major Pond in April of 1886 that he doubted his physical ability to continue performing alone, and he asserted, "I have felt all the time that two congenial men whose work does not conflict, are more than double the attraction that one is. While I could have had a good business by another season alone, it would have been very difficult and disagreeable."[21]

Thus began a four-year business association with Hoosier poet James Whitcomb Riley. Though best known through his books, of course, Riley had achieved some success before audiences reading from his "studies in child-lore and country life."[22] The two men had been friends for a year or so, Nye having visited Riley at the office of the *Indianapolis Journal* when he passed through, and the two had been exchanging letters for a year.[23] In the spring of 1886 Nye and Riley shared a few appearances together under Riley's manager Amos J. Walker. Their first joint reading, which also included Eugene Field, who by this time had become a humorous columnist for the *Chicago Daily News*, was in Indianapolis in February. It was that evening that, to the audience's delight, the noticeably bald Nye was solemnly introduced by Riley as being the "victim of an hereditary affliction that makes him morbidly sensitive . . . —a slight tendency to premature baldness."[24] Nye retaliated by somberly introducing Eugene Field with a request that the audience not use opera glasses on Field since he is "naturally diffident, and since, unlike many of us, he is painfully bald, it will be appreciated as a delicate compliment if the audience will appear not to notice it."[25]

There were a few other Nye-Riley appearances in the spring of 1886, and the team was successful enough to warrant another tour in the fall. But Nye fell ill before the autumn lecture season and had to retreat to the South (Asheville, North Carolina) to regain his health. It was this winter that he was hired as a columnist for the *New York World*, which resulted in his moving to New York in the spring of 1887. He did resume lecturing alone, working out of New York City

in the fall of 1887 (mainly touring New England). Thus, Nye and Riley
did not lecture together that whole 1886–1887 season. In the fall of
1887, however, their appetite for team performances was whetted
when both were asked to appear on a special program in New York's
Chickering Hall on 28–29 November, an event sponsored by the International Copyright League and featuring such writers as James Russell
Lowell, Mark Twain, William Dean Howells, and George Washington
Cable.[26] Riley especially made such a favorable impression with his
reading that his future as a platform "reader" was assured, auguring
well for further Nye-Riley lectures. The pair rode the wake of their
November success into a 15 February 1888 engagement before the
Chicago Press Club and made a minitour of the Chicago area; this was
followed by a return trip to Chickering Hall and a testimonial performance for manager Pond in April.[27] The *Chicago Herald* carried a
sizeable, illustrated review of the 16 February Press Club performance,
praising the two speakers and elaborating on their performances. Of
their evening's work in general the article comments,

The appearance of Bill Nye and James Whitcomb Riley at Central Music
Hall last night, under the auspices of the Chicago Press Club, brought out an
audience that filled the big auditorium. The bald-headed humorist and the
Hoosier poet are the favorites of Chicagoans, who love an occasional bit of
intellectual fun and quaint character-sketching, such as is embodied in Nye's
monologue and Riley's verse, hence there is little to wonder at in the enthusiasm of their reception.

Of Nye specifically, the reviewer writes,

Then Nye came stealing out past the grand piano, and when he reached
the middle of the stage he stopped to remove his eye-glasses and smile. The
outburst of applause that greeted his appearance would have made almost
any other man blush, but the Western humorist simply offered an additional
bow for it, and then he proceeded to tell about the pleasure it afforded him
to play a return engagement "in this house, especially through the agency of
the Chicago Press Club."[28]

The official Nye-Riley partnership was not formed until the fall of
1888, however, when Riley's manager Walker and Nye's manager
Pond reached an agreement and established a corporate managership
of the "Twins of Genius."[29] Pond made out the schedule for 1888–
1889; the two performers, for advertising purposes, wrote spurious
"autobiographies" for each other which Pond circulated; and Riley

hand-decorated the lecture program with humorous drawings.[30] The season was all set, and Nye and Riley opened in Newark, New Jersey, 13 November 1888. Pond was too ill to attend, and attendance was light because the "twins" were relatively unknown, as a team, in the East. Yet they were launched. And after a few humiliating experiences—one house was so nearly empty that Nye refused at first to go on (and the proceeds were only $54)[31]—the pair began attracting large crowds and drawing favorable reviews in the newspapers.

Before the discriminating Boston audience, Major Pond elected to manage the evening's proceedings at Tremont Temple personally. By luck he encountered Mark Twain in a local hotel and persuaded Twain to introduce his team of performers. Pond writes that when Mark appeared on the stage, "the audience rose in a body, and men and women shouted at the very tops of their voices. Handkerchiefs waved, the organist even opened every forte key and pedal in the great organ, and the noise went on unabated for minutes."[32] When the roar quietened, Twain pleased the house by cleverly introducing Nye and Riley as Siamese twins Mr. Eng Nye and Mr. Chang Riley. When the hilarity of Twain's introduction had subsided and Nye, after Riley's appearance, had his turn with the audience, he baited Twain with the following response:

LADIES AND GENTLEMEN,—I am allowed now to speak in a low, familiar tone of voice under the arrangement just made. I cannot do so, however, without saying that, although I have been introduced by this venerable fraud, I fully appreciate the fact that I, though very young and tender, have been introduced by the oldest and the toughest and the best and spiciest of American humorists, a man whose name is not only a household word in America, but also in the Old World, and I forgive him for all of the mean things which he has said, because I know that he is not really so mean as he appears to be. The more you know Mark Twain, the more you associate with him, the more you are compelled to like him, because he really intends to do right; and some day when his hair is all gone there will be under that shock of gray a large two dollar halo, I think. He is really a better man than he looks to be, better than he appears; and both Mr. Riley and I appreciate fully his kindness in coming to Boston and breaking the ice for us to-night, though he has done it in rather an awkward and contemptible way.[33]

The successful appearance of Mark Twain with the two platform newcomers prompted Pond to urge Twain to join the "twins" for an entire tour, but Twain declined.[34]

Nye and Riley's first tour continued with financial and critical suc-

cess until mid-April 1889, when Riley became ill and had to cancel for
the duration of the season. Nye was in such demand as a solo performer, however, that Pond prevailed on him to finish the tour accompanied by a musical group.[35] The second season, 1889–1890, was even
more successful. Pond, ever business-minded, writes that the duo "did
a tremendous business in Washington and in the South. The combination was a more profitable attraction than any opera or theatrical
company."[36] That season was Nye and Riley's last together and Nye's
final one under Pond's managership.

IV   *The Inimitable Pair*

As lecture partners, Nye and Riley were a perfect duo—versatile
and complementary. Their contemporary Melville Landon refers to
their presentation as "the most unique, humorous lecture of the century."[37] Commenting on their typical evening's entertainment—a
mixed bag of Nye's anecdotes and Riley's humorous or sad poems—
Landon continues, "At one time the audience is all in tears at Mr.
Riley's pathos, and then Mr. Nye gets up and sets them screaming with
laughter."[38] Edmund Eitel adds, "There never was such a combination
upon the platform. When the audience had laughed itself weary over
Nye's drollery, Riley led it into a reminiscent or serious mood and
stirred it to impressions and emotions never to be forgotten. . . ."[39]
Nye's part of an evening's fare, Riley's biographer Peter Revell points
out, presented "the satire and grotesquerie of the crackerbarrel tradition, while Riley . . . presented its blander aspects, what Jeannette
Tandy calls its 'matter-of-fact idealism' and 'exuberance.'"[40]
Off stage the relationship between Nye and Riley was mostly congenial. The two friends coached each other "in voice, gesture, posture,
and so forth, that they might be at their best before the footlights."[41]
Mutual friend Eugene Debs, who remembered Nye as a "most lovable
character, kindly, gentle and whole-hearted, and full of innocent fun,"
recalls "an incessant interchange of wit between him and Riley when
they were together. Their contact was mutually infectious and inspir-
iting. . . ."[42] Their friendship led each to praise the other in print, and
Riley confesses even to being with Nye "in fancy" when Nye was
sojourning in Paris in 1889. He writes of sharing all Nye's "sorrows and
. . . joys"[43] while abroad.
Their tours of the two seasons they traveled together under Pond
were lengthy and demanding. Marcus Dickey says of the 1888–1889

season that their circuit "was the most extensive ever spread upon the American map by the Pond Bureau, reaching in time from November to May, and in place from Montgomery, Alabama, to Minneapolis, and from Boston to Portland, Oregon. The tour was to end in Canada."[44] Eitel also recounts that this first tour was to include one hundred dates.[45] But their engagement calendar lists sixty-four dates just for February through April alone.[46] The second season, 1889–1890, spent mainly in the North and Midwest, was grueling in that it included several clusters of "one-night-stands a week." By way of protest, Nye and Riley refused to allow Pond to schedule Sunday performances, called "sacred concerts" by platform lecturers.[47]

Actually, neither season of the Nye-Riley combination was fully completed. In April of 1889, one month before the tour's end, Nye was forced to leave for home because of all four children being stricken with scarlet fever.[48] Riley was the one to defect during the second season when in January 1890, he became too unsettled and ill from alcoholism to finish the season.

Nye's lecture topics were numerous and varied. Usually they were anecdotes or skits, such as his impersonation of a high school girl delivering her graduation essay, the performance Eugene Debs considered one of Nye's "cleverest skits."[49] Or he could make an amusing presentation out of a seemingly pedestrian subject such as farming.[50] When he lectured with Riley, his clever anecdotes and witty observations alternated with Riley's poems.[51] In one of his famous reminiscences, Melville Landon details a Nye-Riley performance much more fully, actually recording the text of each partner's presentation.[52] Nye's part on the program would consist of (1) his "Earth" lecture—a series of both understated and hyperbolic observations about the earth's nature and size plus a facetious look at scientists such as "George Washington Newton"; (2) a travesty on the typical, old-fashioned McGuffy's reader story; (3) his "saw mill" story about the man who backed into the blade (it "took a large chew of tobacco from the plug he had in his pistol pocket and then began on him"); (4) the story of a cunning lad who made money by taking whippings at school; and finally (5) his "cyclone" story, which enumerates several storm disasters which occur after the appearance of a cloud "no larger than a man's hand," a phrase humorously and strategically repeated throughout the telling of the story. Each of these anecdotes would be followed by a Riley poem.

In the second season the Nye-Riley program was expanded to include musicians. An extant souvenir program for 27 January 1890

lists intermittent musical numbers by noted baritone and whistler F.
T. Neely, sensational boy soprano Blatchford Kavanagh, and heralded
pianist Adele Lewing.[53] The printed program carries brief professional
biographies and puffs of these three figures, along with the usual acco-
lades for Nye and Riley. With so much diversity on stage, it is under-
standable why Major Pond advertised the performance as "not a lecture" but an "entertainment."[54]

The Nye-Riley combination lasted until early 1890 when, despite
undaunted success up to that point, circumstances forced an early end
to their professional relationship. Riley had been despondent over having no time to write poetry, he had suffered financially from what was
a poor business stake in the partnership, he was ill in January from
nervous exhaustion, and he began drinking to excess, causing incom-
petence on the platform.[55] Thus the partnership was dissolved in January in Louisville, and Nye finished the season with the musical
accompanists.

Reports of Nye's disloyalty to and slander of Riley circulated in the
press, apparently a smear tactic employed by Riley's original managers, the Western Lyceum Agency. Nye deplored the slander, and Riley
made public testimony to dispel the alleged rift between the two
friends. He called Nye one of his truest friends. "His fealty to me is
beyond all question. We parted friends, as we have always been and
always will be. He understands and I understand. We are wholly congenial, and a better, gentler man I never knew."[56] In a letter to a
friend, written one month after his and Nye's separation, Riley wrote,
"Never have I known a kinder, more considerate or loyal friend or
chum. He said no ill thing of me." Riley went on to blame his managers for the gossip about harsh feelings between the two former partners.[57] For the most part, they did remain friends; but beneath the sur-
face there were some basic conflicts in their professional and personal
relationship that are revealed in Nye's letters to Pond, the humorist
being not so generous with his praise as was Riley.[58] Nye harbored a
number of resentments toward his partner that he apparently disclosed
only in the safety of private correspondence.

Thus the professional relationship that rivaled Mark Twain and
George W. Cable's platform duet ended, each to continue lecturing
and writing independently, and each to go on considering the other his
friend but glad to be free of what had become a somewhat burden-
some joint venture. The "Twins of Genius" might have been "inimitable," as advertised, but they were not indomitable.

V   *The Show Goes On*

Nye did not lecture at all in the fall of 1890. Then for the season of 1891–1892 he left Major Pond's managership and signed with the Redpath Lyceum Bureau in Boston. The contract called for twenty weeks of performances with two weeks of vacation at Christmas.[59] (Nye continued his friendship with and steady stream of letters to Major Pond, and these letters serve as a good source of information on Nye's later career.)

Nye's new manager under Redpath's Bureau, H. B. Thearle, arranged for him to lecture with Alfred P. Burbank, and the two formed a successful partnership that lasted two seasons—1891–1892, 1892–1893—before ending because of Burbank's poor health.[60] Nye and Burbank, advertised anew on red and blue posters as the "Twins of Genius,"[61] proved very compatible personally and professionally and—surprisingly to audiences—were near doubles in looks. Burbank, also lanky and bald, would sometimes be mistaken for Nye on stage and would have to respond to enthusiastic applause by retorting, "'I am not Mr. Nye. I'm the other fellow.'"[62] A surviving lecture program from their tour indicates that Burbank's part on the program consisted primarily of interpretative readings from popular and classical literature.[63] Newspaper reviews were as flattering to Burbank as they were to Nye, emphasizing that Burbank was far more than a mere foil to the more famous performer.[64] Nye enjoyed Burbank's company, as his letters to Pond and his newspaper comments attest. Affectionately dubbing him "Burbie," Nye praised him for being "extremely square in his dealings,"[65] and later wrote, "There never lived a more unselfish gentleman than he. He was not brilliant as an originator, perhaps, but he honestly admitted it, and used to the utmost and best all the powers that God gave him."[66] Nye devoted one newspaper column to a humorous account of Burbank's frustrating struggle, during one of their tours, to sleep in a hotel room with a noisy radiator.[67]

Nye did not lecture in the fall of 1893 because of a trip to England, but in January 1894 he opened with William Hawley Smith of Peoria, Illinois, Burbank now being too ill to tour. Thearle was still the manager. Nye also liked this new partner, calling him "a good man, upright and entertaining too."[68] But his time with Smith was short, January–April 1894, for Nye chose not to lecture the next season but instead spent the winter of 1894–1895 in Washington, D.C., mainly to gather observations on the government for his newspaper columns. In the fall

of 1895 a now visibly ill Nye attempted a last season, and manager
Thearle selected as his partner Bert Poole, cartoonist of the *Boston
Herald*. Poole was to draw cartoons as Nye talked, ludicrously illustrating Nye's subjects and points. The season was disastrous, however,
with Nye being too ill and fatigued to carry the speaking burden alone.
The hitherto enthusiastic audiences failed to react favorably, and Nye
left the platform that fall in disgrace. He would live only a few short
months longer.

    Throughout most of these post-Riley lecture tours, Nye continued to
use the musical acts, working with various singers, pianists, and violin-
ists who provided variety on the program and relief for Nye and his
partner. Occasionally, however, the musical part of the program
brought less than the desired results, as on the night when a group of
small-town people, having misinterpreted the fancy posters announcing Nye and his musical review, came to his show expecting an opera.
Nye muses, "They came arm in arm from the train with bright,
expectant faces to the opera house. Their eyes just danced with expec-
tation. Our manager is to blame for this, for his bills are alive with
pictorial action. He forgets that people who are not profound expect
that the 'attraction' is going to place himself in all these attitudes."[69]
Any number of embarrassing incidents could occur on the circuit.

VI *Platform Manner*

    Nye was a delight on stage in looks, voice, and actions, as well as in
subject matter. The *Colorado Springs Gazette*, reviewing a performance held in the spring of 1890, raved, "Nye is undoubtedly the most
popular humorist and wit to-day before the American public. It is
almost impossible to describe the quaint, original style of the humorist
upon the stage. A person familiar with his writings would know who
was speaking if he should step into the room uninformed as to the character of the entertainment."[70]

    Nye's looks were a humorous technique in themselves. Tall, angular
(until his last few years when he became quite heavy), bald, and often
blank of expression, he prompted inevitable laughter by just shuffling
onto the stage. On one occasion he adorned his face and head with
white makeup seemingly to avoid what Riley noticed as a "bloway and
red" look in the face. Nye applied so much that he looked like a plaster
cast, and when he appeared on stage the audience became "delirious
with joy." "Two ladies in the righthand proscenium box almost fainted

with ill-concealed merriment, and a large, purple man went out into the lobby to laugh."[71] Riley was as overcome by Nye's looks as the audience. The local newspaper the next day exclaimed,

Mr. Nye acquitted himself very gracefully last evening, but added a great deal to the humor of his remarks by making up like Humpty Dumpty. Without a vestige of hair, and completely coated as his entire head and face were with powder, which made his dome of thought look like a white-washed rock in a weary land, he looked so funny that if he had but recited the "Burial of Sir John Moore," people would have more than got their money back.[72]

Nye's humorous remarks were made all the funnier by his serious expression. Only occasionally did the laughter of the audience affect him so much that he would lose his composure. The *Pittsburgh Post* of 18 December 1888 recorded that the previous evening's performance was so joyous that "even Bill smiled in a surprised way, evidently startled at the result of his spontaneous wit. It had escaped him unawares. The bubble was blown unbidden."[73]

His voice was carefully cultivated, and he affected a nasal drawl.[74] Contemporary Mabell Shippie Clarke wrote that "a droll incongruity between word and thought was a part of Mr. Nye's humorous expression, and this incongruity took in conversation the form of a quaintness of speech that possessed an infinite charm for the listener."[75] Nye's publisher, J. B. Lippincott, spoke of the "deliberate" pace of Nye's voice, observing that it "had a distinct ring of melancholy in it—a characteristic peculiar to many professional humorists."[76] Riley perhaps best characterized his partner's original and indescribable voice when he wrote to a friend, "Nye is simply superb on the stage—and no newspaper report can half-way reproduce either the curious charm of his drollery—his improvisations—inspirations and so forth. At times his auditors are hysterical with delight."[77]

Exaggerated gestures often accompanied the unemotional voice, the resulting incongruity being another of Nye's humorous methods. As early as 1880, when Nye was in Laramie and making political speeches for Republican candidates for office, his gestures were a noticeable part of his delivery. The *Minneapolis Tribune* credited his unique success as a speaker to his style of gesturing, humorously claiming that listeners who sat the fence were doubtful over what to fear the most—"'the success of an unprincipled Democracy or the frolicsome gestures of the speaker'" ("The Secret Of Garfield's Election," *NB*, 264). The *Still-*

water Lumberman quipped, "'The speech last evening was noticeable for its grandeur of conception and the picturesque grace of its calisthentics. . . . Toward the close of the speech when Mr. Nye got warmed up to his work, and seemed to be lost in a wilderness of dissolving limbs, the police interfered and prevented the sacrifice of human life'" (*NB*, 264). The *Clear Lake News* spoke of Nye's gestures as "'imported at great expense for his own use,'" and "'death-dealing'" to an unsafe audience (*NB*, 265).

Addressing the antics of Nye's comic lectures, the *Chicago Herald* said that his speech alone is sufficient cause for his being famous, "but his postures are something far more grotesque."[78] An illustrator of the same review attempted to capture Nye in six caricatures of his stage stance. With his exotic gymnastic poses, Nye resembles respectively a praying mantis, a spider, and a monkey. His unorthodox gestures were sometimes combined with clownish stage antics, such as his reading a Riley poem by ducking into the wings after each stanza only to be coaxed out gradually by the audience's laughter and applause.[79] His wild gesturings could be comically emphasized by trembling hands encased in white gloves.[80] And, of course, his angular frame, which appeared to be all arms and legs, made his gestures all the more pronounced.

All of these carefully cultivated humorous techniques would have meant little, of course, were it not for suitable material. Eitel reminds us of the effective, if absurd and ridiculous, anecdotes which Nye delivered to his audiences.[81] A *Colorado Springs Gazette* reviewer praised Nye's dry wit, punning that the intemperate Riley could not travel with him any longer it was so dry; that wit "proved most fascinating to the audience, and his every appearance was an ovation."[82] Perhaps all of Nye's talents and techniques as a stage humorist are best summed up in Riley's appraisal of his partner:

> The quaintness and whimsicality of Mr. Nye's humor was the notable thing about him. It was unaccountable upon any particular theory. It just seemed natural for his mind to work at that gait. He recognized the matter-of-fact view others took of the general proposition of life, and sympathized with it, but he did so with a native tendency to surprise and astound that ordinary state of mind and vision. He could say a ridiculous thing or perpetuate a ridiculous act with a face like a Sphinx, knowing full well that those who saw or heard would look to his face for some confirmation of their suspicion that it was time to laugh. They had to make up their minds about it unaided by him, however, for they never found any trace of levity in his countenance. As he would say, he did his laughing "elsewhere."[83]

VII A *Sweet Yet Thorny Road*

There were many advantages to being a successful platform lecturer. The financial reward, as in Nye's case, could be outstanding,[84] the travel enlightening and exciting, appreciative audiences gratifying and stimulating. Nye usually enjoyed the various types of people he met on the trains, found each hotel a new experience, if not a challenge, and joked about such matters as the hoard of hotel keys he had accrued ("A Collection of Keys," *R*, 383–84). He often entertained himself and amused his fellow train passengers by resorting to a number of clever tricks. At a station stop he would seize the round leather sofa pillows from the smoking car, stuff one under each arm, and stroll the platform with pillow tassels dangling, obviously attracting curious stares from the crowd. Another favorite stunt was to read aloud imaginary signs as the train rolled into a station, causing other passengers to crane their necks in an effort to see for themselves. When train boys would pass through the cars selling books, Nye would snatch one, read aloud a totally fabricated story that was wholly out of keeping with the contents of the book, then straightfacedly hand the volume back to the astonished peddler, who would go off and search the pages carefully for the story Nye had "read."[85]

Responsive audiences, of course, were a great pleasure to Nye. He found them in many places; in fact, he observed that no section of the country was more receptive than the others. But he felt the best audience for enthusiasm is "a young audience, a college audience or an audience of teachers or newspaper men. . . ."[86] Detroit and Pittsburgh were among his favorite cities in which to perform and enjoy enthusiastic listeners. The *Pittsburgh Dispatch* reported, after one Nye-Riley performance:

"Fun and merriment reigned in various stages the whole evening, principally the superlative stage. The faces of the audience in the different contortions that the excessive mirth produced, were a side-splitting study in themselves. The hall was taxed to the utmost to accommodate the laughingly shaking mass of humanity. Round after round and peal after peal of applause and laughter, greeted the humorists at every move, word and look."[87]

Supposedly after the hall emptied that night, "'the janitor swooped around and gathered up a quart of buttons.'"[88] When Nye was elated over audience reaction, he would write Pond or his *New York World* employers about it, or mention it in his newspaper columns. He occasionally sought out and thanked a single benefactor, as in his Sunday article on 9 April 1893, after a California performance: "P. S.—Thanks are hereby extended to Isaac W. Ford, who attended our performance at San Bernardino and laughed heartily during the evening."[89]

If Mark Twain spoke of the "trouble beginning at 8:00," Nye would quickly agree, though adding that trouble was fairly constant. Commenting on the difficulties of lecturing, he wrote,

The lecturer has two or three great obstacles to overcome which the actor has not, viz., he has no scenery, he has to occupy the entire evening alone, and there is no division into three or four acts, with a chance for the audience to rest and run down the show. And yet the lecturer often starts out fearlessly without training, or with training that is far worse than none, and on the reputation he has made in some totally different art he fearlessly rushes in where angels would naturally hang back and advertises to lecture. At the expense of the public he thus, if persistent and brave, at last learns to be natural—if he didn't foolishly get his originality and individuality trained out of him by a journeyman elocutionist on the start—and is then considered a professional. He can think of other more interesting topics than his speech and sit himself down by the roadside of life at times to calmly remove the thorns and brambles from his tired feet—thorns and brambles accumulated all along the harsh and fiercely thorny road over which he has traveled toward even a moderate success.[90]

The disadvantages of lecturing were indeed many, and often severe. The fatigue of travel and the pinched schedule of one-night stands took their toll on Nye, not a robust man to begin with. He began to find lecturing irksome fairly early in his career, commenting to Major Pond in February 1888: "All the western managers want to 'handle' me which indicates that they are making money. *But* I am quite doubtful whether I will make a show of myself any more. *I dislike it beyond all description* [my italics]. It may be gratifying to some and surely if it be pleasant to be feted and fed and wined and dined and fired from one end of the country to the other, I ought to be happy, but I do not pant for that kind of joy."[91]

The strain of the circuit was especially heavy on Nye, not only because of his fragile health but also because of his simultaneous obligation to write a weekly newspaper column. He complained to Major Pond in 1890, "With 5 nights a week I would not have felt so tired of it but you know that my contract to write each week could not be broken and so I've had double duty to perform."[92]

Travel schedules and arrangements proved most difficult at times.

There were extensive layovers between trains;[93] arrivals in the wrong towns with trunks sometimes sent elsewhere;[94] drafty or overheated or noisy hotels to put up in; local arrangements committees to tolerate and please by accepting offers of guided tours through uninteresting towns.[95] Nye complained in one of his columns,

Here [in America] one tears himself away from an audience that has just learned to love him, and changing his evening dress in the cab on his way to the 10:40 train rides till 2:30 A. M., gets out at a junction where there is a well and a liberty pole and waits two hours for a way freight, on which he rides all day, eating what the engineer doesn't want, and at 7 o'clock he drops fainting into the arms of an old acquaintance who wants to take him out to his country home in a cutter. The thermometer is 20 odd, or at least it would be 20 odd if it had not been that way for three weeks and ceased to be odd.[96]

Nye was saddled with the additional problem, for a few years, of having to fend for Riley, who could not read a railroad schedule or figure out connections and who harbored a constant fear of boarding the wrong train (which indeed would happen when Nye was not at his side to assist).[97]

There could also be exasperating difficulties with managers in working out reasonable schedules,[98] problems in getting pay from local agents, woes from unfriendly audiences and hostile newspaper reviews,[99] loneliness and anxiety from traveling and lecturing alone,[100] and even unexpected dangers to encounter in the theater itself. In Yazoo, Mississippi, for example, Nye stepped out an upstairs door the landing to which had been removed; he broke his arm and was badly shaken and bruised.[101] His general ennui and disgust with the trials of the stage prompted such comments as, "I think it's a good idea to reform and abandon such a life before the hearse is actually at the door waiting for one. I am cheerily preparing to say farewell to these triumphal tours which wreck both soul and body at so much a pair."[102]

In sum, Nye had to share the sweets of the circuit—the high pay, good times, warm audiences—with the bitter. In many ways the circuit attracted and repulsed him simultaneously, and perhaps his final view of the stage is contained in these ambivalent remarks from two essays on lecturing:

Lecturers are better treated on the whole now than twenty years ago, and the eggs used by those who criticized the performance are of a higher order of excellence, it seems to me.[103]

The history of the lecture industry of America is one of alternate elation and depression. It is a history of alternate failure and success, written with the heart's blood of the lecturer. It is a record of hope and indigestion, of exhilarating applause and nipping frosts.[104]

VIII   *From Stage to Page*

Nye's lecturing career so exercised all his talents and efforts that it had a major impact on his writings. As mentioned above, the lecturing ran simultaneously with his newspaper career. Travel and countless stage experiences so broadened him that the columns he wrote while a lecturer became much more varied, vigorous, and fully developed than his early ones in the Western papers. And he drew on his platform experiences to embellish many a column during the last ten years of his life, 1886–1896.

In addition, two of Nye's books specifically evince stage influence, one being a direct product of Nye and Riley's lecture partnership. And a third volume resulted from the success and popularity of the two partners. It has already been mentioned in chapter 2 that the book *Remarks* (1887), written when Nye had left the West and settled back in Wisconsin for a few years, contained much longer, more fully developed pieces than the earlier *Bill Nye and Boomerang, Forty Liars,* and *Baled Hay.* One reason for this added development was that by the time Nye wrote *Remarks* he had been introduced to the stage and had, thus, been forced to learn how to develop and sustain a topic more extensively. Many of the essays and sketches in *Remarks* are materials Nye actually developed for platform presentation, and others reflect experiences relating to the stage.[105]

A popular type of book at the time was the "railroad reader," a volume designed for the entertainment and/or information of the rail traveler. Having frequently ridden trains to meet lecture engagements and seen how these books were consumed by the public, Nye and Riley conceived the idea of writing one themselves. Though it was not published until 1888, the partners were at work on it by the end of their first season of joint lecturing. On 5 April 1886 Nye wrote Riley, "I have nearly completed the *Introduction* for our R. R. guide,"[106] and Riley responded enthusiastically two days later, "There's not an hour of the day I'm not thinking of that venture—and more and more convinced that it'll stanch a long-felt want, and we can hustle it into market, too, before any long delay. That's the beauty of it—it really wants to look impromptu—and be so—measurably so, at least."[107]

When the book appeared, late in 1888, it sold for one dollar in cloth and fifty cents in paper. Reviewers were laudatory, the *Book Buyer* referring to its "mirth-provoking qualities" and commenting that "the humor of Nye's sketches, like that of James Whitcomb Riley's verse, is of a peculiar kind, and has a unique relish."[108]

The book consists of 203 pages of Nye's essays, sketches, and anecdotes, along with poems by Riley. The text is profusely and cleverly illustrated by Baron De Grimm, Eugene Zimmerman, and Walt McDougall, to mention the major artists represented. In their preface, "Why It Was Done," the authors announce their intentions and chart the difference between their railway guide and others:

What this country needs, aside from a new Indian policy and a style of poison for children which will be liable to kill rats if they eat it by accident, is a Railway Guide which will be just as good two years ago as it was next spring—a Railway Guide if you please, which shall not be cursed by a plethora of facts, or poisoned with information—a Railway Guide that shall be rich with doubts and lighted up with miserable apprehensions. In other Railway Guides, pleasing fancy, poesy and literary beauty, have been throttled at the very threshold of success, by a wild incontinence of facts, figures, asterisks and references to meal stations. For this reason a guide has been built at our own shops and on a new plan. It is the literary *piece de resistance* of the age in which we live. It will not permit information to creep in and mar the reader's enjoyment of the scenery. It contains no railroad map which is grossly inaccurate. It has no time table in it which has outlived its uselessness. It does not prohibit passengers from riding on the platform while the cars are in motion. It permits everyone to do just as he pleases and rather encourages him in taking that course.

The authors of this book have suffered intensely from the inordinate use of other guides, having been compelled several times to rise at 3 o'clock A. M. in order to catch a car which did not go and which would not have stopped at the station if it had gone.

They have decided, therefore, to issue a guide which will be good for one to read after one has missed one's train by reason of one's faith in other guides which we may have in one's luggage. (*RG*, xi–xii)

With their plea, then, of being "wholly irresponsible, and . . . glad of it," the two offer a carefree string of contents designed to help the traveler rest his mind from the frustrating details and pesky inconveniences of railroad travel.

Despite Riley's appearance in the volume by way of thirty-four poems, the book is far more Nye's than his. Nye's sketches both begin and end the volume, and many of the pieces are autobiographical or

personal in some way, thus providing the reader much more of a feel
for Nye than Riley. Nye's very first sketch, "Where He First Met His
Parents," the opening selection of the book, provides an immediate
contact with the droll, candid Nye that lingers throughout the volume.
Of his twenty-five entries, a dozen had appeared in 1887–1888 as Sunday columns in his writing for the *New York World*. The other thirteen
he seems to have composed specifically for the *Railway Guide*. The
pieces are typical Nye fare, the kinds of essays, sketches, and anecdotes
found in his books and newspaper columns after the early Western
period. The largest portion, eight in all, relate autobiographical or personal experiences and philosophy; four deal with famous personages
(two with Jay Gould, one with Julius Caesar, one with Methuselah).
There are three poignant character sketches: "The Chemist Of The
Carolinas" (about a moonshiner), "The Diary of Darius T. Skinner"
(a braggart bumpkin in New York), and a sad piece about a drunken
newspaper editor who has been deserted by his wife ("Our Wife").
Two sketches concern the sport of fox hunting. Otherwise, there is a
typical Nye burlesque (on newspaper social columns), a play review,
a travel account (of Niagara Falls), an animal essay (on the Tar-heel
cow), an account of an experience with a fortune-teller, and a sympathetic essay on agriculture ("Her Tired Hands"). Two narratives—
a parody of an old-fashioned McGuffey's reader story and a surprisingly serious (for Nye) Christmas narrative ("The Rise And Fall Of
William Johnson")—round out Nye's share of the contents.

   Undoubtedly the most interesting pieces by Nye are the two narratives and the eight personal anecdotes. The latter include Nye's
account of his youth and boyhood home ("Where He First Met His
Parents"), his acceptance of an honorary membership in a farmer's
club ("A Letter Of Acceptance"), a facetious disclaimer of his candi-
dacy for president ("Healthy But Out Of The Race"), letters of application for a railroad job ("Lines On Turning Over A Pass"), a plaintive
open letter begging the return of the Nyes' defected chambermaid
("'Oh, Willhelmina, Come Back!'"), an account of a layover in a small-
town hotel ("Where The Roads Are Engaged In Forking"), an essay
on sleeping and snoring ("A Blasted Snore"), a humorous protest over
a newspaper story that confused Nye's house in Staten Island with a
new hospital ("Seeking To Set The Public Right"), and a complaint
about his being judged with suspicion by strangers encountering him
for the first time ("Seeking To Be Identified").

   Most of these eight vignettes depict Nye in ludicrous light and bear examples of his pointed wit and satire, mainly with himself as target. He tells the farmer's club in Massachusetts that he will gladly be an honorary member, but he will deliver no speeches and do no judging at the county fair: "After a person has had a fountain pen kicked endwise through his chest by the animal to which he has awarded the prize, and later on has his features worked up into a giblet pie by the owner of the animal to whom he did not award the prize, he does not ask for public recognition at the hands of his fellow citizens" (*RG*, 39). In "Healthy But Out Of The Race," the qualifications he lists for office all point to himself—a candidate who is "a plain man, a magnetic but hairless patriot" (*RG*, 80)—and Nye will be awaiting, as he works in his cellar with his potatoes, the nomination by acclamation. In "Seeking To Set The Public Right," after Nye has assured readers that his house is not really the opulent building the reporter thought, he draws a sketch of his abode—a rude cabin—and quips, "Of course I have idealized it somewhat, but only in order to catch the observant reader. The front part of the house runs back to the time of Polypus the First, while the L, which does not show in the drawing, runs back as far as the cistern"(*RG*, 186). In "Seeking To Be Identified," Nye muses over why people react to him with such suspicion, telling a comic incident of not being allowed to deposit money in a bank until he proved his identity; he showed a copy of the *New York World* containing his likeness in caricature, and immediately the teller hastily closed the door of the safe and spun the combination (*RG*, 199–200). The comic pose continues in such manner through all eight personal pieces in *Railway Guide*. Again, as mentioned earlier, Nye found that using himself as the butt of a joke was a valuable key to making his humor successful.

When the *Railway Guide* was in press, Riley wrote Nye, "I just pray for the success of that book; and if it does succeed—we've got a little jersey mine, and one of the very pleasantest ones to work in the world."[109] Popular it was, enjoying six reprintings under various titles from 1889 to 1905.[110] But Riley's prayers for financial success went unanswered, for apparently he and Nye had agreed to a poor business arrangement with their publisher. Over a year later the two were trying to find copies of any legal documents which could be used to demand more money, but they were unsuccessful.[111] The whole financial fiasco was sometimes told by Riley in the form of a humorous story; he depicted the Dearborn Publishing Company as "Ketchem & Skinem" of Chicago, and jested that the only pay the two authors received was a hundred shares apiece in the company, "and the company never paid any dividends before it went out of business."[112]

A final publication resulting from the Nye-Riley partnership appeared five years after Nye's death. In 1901 the W. B. Conkey Company of Chicago brought out *Nye and Riley's Wit and Humor: Amusing Prose Sketches and Quaint Dialect Poems*, reprinted the next year by the Homewood Publishing Company. The book actually reflects no influence of Nye's stage career, however, for the Nye portion—which is all but ten of the 544 pages—consists of reprinted essays and sketches from three of his earlier books, *Bill Nye and Boomerang, Forty Liars*, and *Bill Nye's Chestnuts, Old and New*. It is an appealing volume containing some of Nye's best vintage pieces, but it does not merit separate discussion since the works all appear in other books treated in detail in this study.

CHAPTER 5

The World Calls: Nye in New York

WHEN Nye's poor health caused a temporary halt to his lecturing with James Whitcomb Riley in the fall of 1886, he moved South for a winter of convalescence to Asheville, North Carolina. His expectations of a warm Southern winter were squelched, however, when in early December an unusually heavy snowstorm covered the Asheville area. In jest Nye wrote a humorous reaction to the storm, facetiously postmarking the sketch "In My Sunny Southern Home," and sent it to the *New York World* for possible publication. He drew his own illustration for the article, a wintry scene featuring a snow-covered cabin nestled in blanketed hills, with Nye himself—dressed in heavy jacket with large mittens and earmuffs—standing in the snow before his cabin, shovel in hand: "I write these lines from the South. I came here in order to evade the severe winters of the North. I have tried to show in the inclosed sketch how I appear while in the act of evading the severe winter of the extreme North. It is, of course, only a rough draught, but that was the kind of draught we were having when I made the sketch."[1] The essay includes typical examples of Nye's humorous anticlimax, such as "In the house there is a case of Budweiser beer and a case of croup," and "This region is noted for its Christmas trees, rhododendrons and rheumatism."[2]

The essay made a hit with *World* owner Joseph Pulitzer and managing editor Colonel John A. Cockerill, who immediately recognized Nye's abilities and potential as a popular columnist and offered him a position as weekly writer on their famous paper. In signing with Cockerill and Pulitzer, Nye was embarking on a venture that would result in ten illustrious years as a columnist for major American newspapers from coast to coast.

I Rise to World Fame

Though the *World* offer was appealing to Nye, he had qualms about leaving the South and fears about moving to New York City. As E. J. Edwards states,

He felt that it would be a dangerous thing for a humorist to go to New York City. He doubted whether such a person could maintain himself there, and he believed that the chances were that in the whirl of newspaper life, and especially of a newspaper conducted at such high pressure as is The World, the humorist would be stunned, his work would become forced and artificial, his identity would be lost, and he would sink to the dead level of the average.[3]

Nevertheless, Nye worked out a satisfactory arrangement with the World. He would be able to write what he pleased for his weekly column, he would not be subject to a regular office routine at the newspaper's headquarters, he would have free rein to publish in magazines, and he would receive $150 a week base pay plus whatever he could make from other newspapers and magazines (and, of course, from his lecturing).[4] Under those terms, he went to New York in the spring of 1887, and eventually settled with his family into a fashionable, commodious house, which Nye termed their "Slosh," at Tompkinsville on Staten Island.[5]

Nye soon became famous for his Sunday World column. The fears he had harbored of not being enthusiastically received by the metropolitan reading audience proved groundless. His Sunday visit with World readers became so popular that the editors were usually careful to print explanatory notes on Sundays when, for reasons of illness or travel, Nye's "letter" did not appear. His popularity was enhanced by the clever illustrations drawn by World caricaturist Walter McDougall. Apparently Pulitzer and Cockerill conceived of the idea for the comic illustrations from Nye's own rough caricature which accompanied the "Sunny Southern Home" spoof.[6] McDougall's sketches added so much to Nye's humor that he continued to illustrate the columns throughout most of Nye's remaining years of writing for newspapers, there being only intermittent periods when Nye's sketches were not illustrated. McDougall's caricature of Nye—a tall, grotesquely stringy figure with skinny neck supporting a completely bald, gourd-shaped head—became so well known that Nye was often readily identified wherever he went even without being introduced. McDougall enjoyed telling the story of drawing the patented comic portrait of Nye on an envelope, simply writing "New York" on it, and mailing it: "so well was his face known that he received the letter the next morning, much to his own astonishment."[7] And the night Nye powdered his head before stepping onto the lecture stage, causing a close resemblance to McDougall's caricature, his appearance stirred

"a thrill of recognition that was delightful to my own vanity,"
McDougall also recalled.[8]

Nye and McDougall became close friends and traveling companions,
McDougall often accompanying Nye on his travels for the *World*.
Seven years after Nye's death, McDougall reminisced about his
deceased friend and associate, saying,

> Of the many men with whom I have been fairly intimate there is not one
> who has worn so well, for whom an honest admiration has increased rather
> than lessened with intimacy. . . .
> I have made fun of him in the most ridiculous ways I could devise in my
> pictures, yet with a loving and admiring hand that lingered always over his
> gentle, strong face, whose every line I know by heart.[9]

Nye himself, certainly not displeased with the image McDougall had
created of him, commented,

> Everywhere I go I find people who seem pleased with the manner in which
> I have succeeded in resembling the graphic pictures made to represent me in
> the "World." I can truly say that I am not a vain man, but it is certainly
> pleasing and gratifying to be greeted by a glance of recognition and a yell of
> genuine delight from total strangers. . . .
> These pictures also stimulate the press of the country to try it themselves
> and to add other horrors which do not in any way interfere with the likeness,
> but at the same time encourage me to travel mostly by night.[10]

II World *Traveler*

One of the most rewarding aspects of Nye's position with the *World*
was the opportunity to travel occasionally as a correspondent. These
trips were different from Nye's fatiguing lecture travels, for they
afforded him time to collect himself and even enjoy some leisure while
he was gathering observations for his columns. One trip took him to
Paris for several weeks in June 1889 to cover the World Exposition;
afterward he visited London.

Nye's travel accounts are among his most interesting and entertaining newspaper writings. A key to their success is Nye's continued
emphasis on the human element. Rarely does he devote a column to
blanket description of sights and scenes of foreign locales; there are
always people and interesting human events. Characteristically, Nye
himself often remains the butt of most of the humor. In Paris, aside

from calling the city lively ("I read in a book many years ago that Paris was a very gay city, and I thought then that if I ever visited the place personally I would speak of that feature")[11] and boasting about strolling the "Chong Eliza,"[12] he mainly concentrates on such human interest features as the presence of Buffalo Bill and his wild West show,[13] visiting a museum and almost being locked in as "an extra freak in the collection" because of dozing off while sitting and daydreaming in an antique carriage,[14] and being arrested for allegedly breaking a drinking glass at a sidewalk cafe (Nye was innocent).[15] In London, on that same 1889 trip, he writes of meeting Bret Harte at a reception and jestingly reproaching Harte "for some remarks once made by him to build up his own reputation at the expense of mine. I do not play euchre, especially with a Chinaman, and I made him admit right there before every one that he did not mean any disrespect"[16] (in creating the card shark Nye in his famous poem "Plain Language From Truthful James").

III   Nye in Gotham: A Potpourri of Interests

Though Nye had misgivings about living in New York, his writings reflect marked expansion of his interests and knowledge as a result of his sojourning there. He branched out into areas he had never had occasion to explore. Moreover, his thinking on other subjects reached a maturity and sophistication not evident in his earlier—especially the Western—writings.

New York City itself is a major subject of Nye's columns for the *World*. He poured out his observations on nature in Central Park (especially *human* nature), Wall Street economics, the wretched administration of the New York Customs House, recreation at Coney Island and Long Branch, local baseball games and boxing matches, and the virtues of Staten Island versus Manhattan. He satirized the social gamut of peoples in the area, from the elite "Four Hundred" comfortably listed in Ward McAllister's social register to the lowly Harlemites often stuck with intolerable living conditions.[17] He jests that the reason he himself is not included in McAllister's favored band is his trade background: "Why did I ever tell Mac that my father hauled flour to Galena?"[18] In actuality, as might be expected, Nye felt the "Four Hundred" were "jackasses."[19]

Certainly Nye became thoroughly familiar with the city, as his writings show, and he grew fond of Staten Island. But the numerous prob-

lems of this settlement of about two million people oppressed him and
caused him to reaffirm his position as a rural man who for a time was
dwelling in New York as an observer. Manhattan he considered to be
corrupt and dirty,[20] frightfully expensive, congested, and incommo-
dious. He marveled that New Yorkers not only suffered all the hardships but never even considered moving elsewhere:

> The solemn truth is . . . that there is at present a fraction over two millions
> of people in New York this fall who would rather suffer and kick and wail
> and whoop and be spattered with mud by loose car-rails, insulted by brutal
> guards, disembowelled by umbrellas under the arms of tall intellectual warts,
> spitted by the canes of those who get ahead of the multitude and back up,
> with their sticks aimed at the umbillicus of a long suffering people; neglected
> by the un-"seen" waiter, skun by the un-"seen" barber, robbed by the hack-
> man, brained by the policeman, blown up by the steam heating company,
> skinned by the papers, stank to death by the gas leak and the peach orchard
> sewer system, stung to death by remorse, fricasseed to death by nude electric
> wires, crushed by the crowds, nauseated by the nuisances, killed by the cars,
> disfigured by the truck-drivers, crazed by commerce, shot by mistake,
> gnawed by mad dogs, dogged by detectives, accosted by unknown ladies late
> at night who ought to be far away in some quiet dell weeding onions instead
> of going about in a thickly settled community after eating them; watched by
> watchmen, butchered by butchers, burgled by burglars, fugled by fuglers for-
> ever, than live in any other city they know of at half the expense and twice
> the salary.[21]

But like the city or not, Nye was astute enough to take advantage of
its cultural and business advantages. On the latter score, he even exercised his real estate interest by purchasing a flat in Manhattan.[22]

If anything, Nye's portraiture of famous living persons greatly pro-
liferated during the years he wrote for the *World*. Boss Tweed, Horace
Greeley, Dr. Mary Walker, Frederick Remington, Robert Ingersol, the
Astor family, and Jay Gould are only some of the illustrious names that
lace his columns. Nye was particularly fascinated with Gould, as he
would become with George Vanderbilt in North Carolina later. Nye
fabricated a friendship between himself and "the Little King" (in one
sketch they are haying and chasing hornets together on Gould's Irving-
ton farm)[23] and wrote a whole series of articles on their relationship
and on various aspects of Gould's life—all satirical, of course. Despite
Nye's skepticism of the values represented by the financial barons of
his day, he could not help but be awed by them, in part because—like
Mark Twain—he revered financial success and longed for it personally.

The *World* columns reflect Nye's growing interest in sports, science, and art. He developed an enthusiasm for horse racing and baseball, though he mocked baseball journalism.[24] Toward boxing he was more ambivalent, though he zealously denigrated John L. Sullivan in his article on the pugilist as "litterateur."[25] The interest in science and technology led him to write columns on astronomy, a Carolina chemist, electricity, and the future of the human race,[26] the latter a science fiction article which humorously charts the physical and mental changes the human race will undergo as custom and invention make their imprint.

Nye had long been interested in art, toying with illustrations himself and thinking about the nature of art. As early as the 1884 essay "Incongruity" (*BH*, 282–83), he mocked an artist who mistakenly drew a frying pan instead of a gold pan to illustrate a Western mining scene, admonishing, "The artist should study as far as possible to imitate nature and not make a fool of himself" (*BH*, 283). From both living in New York and traveling for the *World*, he often found himself close to famous art collections, which he visited and then discussed in his Sunday columns. Sometimes his reactions were purely playful, satiric, and deliberately naive, such as in his column on visiting the New York Academy of Design to view an exhibition of paintings from Paris. After remarking that "many of these pictures are large and beautiful, while others are small and ornery," Nye proceeds to describe various individual masterpieces, claiming that a Charles Durand is poorly executed because the artist leaves the viewer in doubt as to whether the female subject of the painting is intoxicated, and appraising a work by Pissaro as "worth $3 of any man's money, for the frame is worth $2, and there is at least a dollar's worth of paint on the picture that is just as good as ever."[27]

Philistine, then, he sometimes was, scoffing at the pretensions of good art. Not always, however. He obviously took art far more seriously than his satiric barbs imply; he even became enough of an art enthusiast to indulge in some collecting. In a column written two years later than the satiric one just examined, Nye praises Rochester, New York, for its "notable" art gallery, which is "worth a journey of some length to visit." He describes a tour of "this fine aggregation of beautiful pictures," his acquaintance with the director of the museum, and the characteristics of painters from Rubens to Titian. His comments on the paintings are largely serious and provocative,[28] as they are in a later column written while Nye was in England for the second time in

1893.[29] He made it a point to visit the National Gallery on the day
when the copyists came to emulate the old masters. After closely
observing the copyists at work—in fact, so closely he was asked to leave
them to work without interruption—Nye discusses the work of Turner
and Hogarth, neither of whom he likes. Turner, he says, is not appreciated by the common man, though "Artists never speak severely of
him." Nye confesses, "I do not care for him. . . . If you will give me a
good, clean tablecloth and move it around a little each meal so that the
place where I carve will come on a new spot each time, I'll give you
in a week's time a Turner that by touching up a little will make people
pop their eyes out." He notes with little surprise that no artists are
copying in the Hogarth room: "His portrait of himself, by himself,
hung where it faced his 'Marriage a la Mode' on the opposite wall, and
he seemed to say to himself sadly, 'Did I devote my inspired brush to
such work as that and hope to be loved or copied in coming years?'"[30]
Nye obviously disliked stark realism in art, but he also had trouble with
impressionism. His tastes ran to the middle ground in painting between
the extremes of representationalism and nonrepresentationalism. He
particularly appreciated portraiture in art, not a surprising fact considering that his chief interest in life was people.

IV *"A Great Bookworm"*

Nye's interest in the literary world also seemed to reach its height
during the New York period when he was closest to the world of publishers and writers. His *World* columns frequently touch on a range of
literary subjects, from copyright laws to the lives of famous authors of
his day. Nye became involved in the literary scene as both critic and
practitioner.

His own creative talents embraced both prose and poetry. As we
have seen in his early books, his penchant for writing fiction was especially strong. Anecdotal bagatelles and burlesque narratives abound in
his early books, and narratives comprise occasional newspaper columns. For example, one column is a parody of Southern local color
fiction of the Charles Egbert Craddock school of writing.[31] The main
target of Nye's fictional burlesques was romanticized fiction. He pre-
ferred realism. In an early essay entitled "Fiction" (*FL*, 226–29) he
comments favorably on the changes from romantic to realistic fiction
as reflected in character, plot, style, and tone in each type of writing.
The heroes of romances—"languid young gentlemen who do not have

to work"—have rightfully given way to the realistic portraiture of recent fiction where there are people "who wear overcoats and ulsterettes when it is cold, and who eat, and get vaccinated, and quarrel, and lie abed in the morning, and act like the balance of mankind" (FL, 227–28). Love stories, he points out in a late newspaper column, should feature not only star-struck youth but widowers too: "Why not give the carroty widower a show in song and fiction—a 'wadower' fifty-three years old and sixteen hands high."[32]

Nye's enjoyment of poetry did not lag far behind his preference for fiction. He not only wrote poetry and commented on the process but also theorized in general on the nature of poetry. The few poems he wrote are scattered throughout his books and newspaper columns. Some of them, quite frankly, are silly, contrived verses (e.g., "Ode to Spring," NB, 87; "Ode to the Cucumber," FL, 157). Others, however, show surprising skill. Nye could be clever with burlesque poetry. "Footsteps" is in part a parody on Longfellow's "A Psalm of Life":

> Years ago the poet told us we could
>   Make our lives sublime,
> And departing, leave behind us
>   Footprints on the sands of time—
>
> Footprints that perhaps another,
>   Sailing o'er life's stormy main,
> Some forlorn and shipwrecked brother,
>   Seeing, might take heart again.
>
> Ah, the footsteps of my mother!
>   How they shaped my early course!
> How they steered me and me brother
>   With their strong yet gentle force!
>
> Now my days are swiftly fleeing,
>   But the memory naught can shake
> Of those footsteps on my being
>   That her slipper used to make.[33]

A poem on a North Carolina drought, written after Nye had left New York to return South, provides a humorous slant to the stanza form and rhythm of Stephen Foster's "My Old Kentucky Home." Entitled "Midsummer On My Place At A Given Point, And Looking Toward Roan Mountain Between The Stanzas," the poem reads,

I.

Oh, the sweet potato's swelling on my upright farm,
    And the sourwood blossom feeds the bee,
And Kope Elias with his strong right arm
    Scoots the moonshine maker up a tree.

II.

Oh, the sun shines hot on my blue-grass lawn,
    And the mule goes on mighty sad,
For my upright farm is a dark Venetian red,
    And the eating clay is looking mighty bad.

III.

For my lawn is as red as the sandy-bottom road,
    And the peach busts open on the bough,
And my long parch-ed well at the back of my abode
    Wants a cold, damp towel on its brow.

IV.

It never was so droughty since prior to the war,
    When the apples got so wormy on the tree,
And it puzzled you all to know what they was for,
    Except a gnurly death for you and me.

V.

But the banks may bust 'n do the money centers
    harm,
    I reck not a low-neck clam,
For I am content on my upright farm,
    And that's why I seem like I am.[34]

(And then, of course, there is the effective mock-heroic "Apostrophe To An Orphan Mule," the first stanza of which is quoted in chapter 2.) Nye's ingenious feel for language and seemingly innate sense of rhythm and timing could have led to more satisfactory poetic productivity had his bent not been primarily burlesque and had his tastes been more fully developed. His thoughts on poetry were serious ones, and he realized his own limitations:

It is not often that I drop into rhyme, but where I can thus express a great truth, and in that form, I may be pardoned perhaps for doing so. I do not idealize so much in my verse, but prefer rather to express with great force some grand ideas.

I love nature, as all true poets must, and would be glad to paint a rhythmic picture with the verbal colorings of a Byron, but that is not wherein my great gift lies. I am better fitted to write in a spirited yet direct and descriptive way, and should be classed more in the group of poets to which Bryant belonged. Bryant was a practical man and even thrifty and economical.[35]

Nye sharply criticized popular poets of the Julia A. Moore school, deploring their rampant use and violation of poetic license: "A poetic license, as I understand it, simply allows the poet to jump the 15 over the 14 in order to bring in the proper rhyme, but it does not allow the writer to usurp the management of the entire system of worlds, and introduce dog-days and ice-cream between Christmas and New Year . . ." ("The Muse," *NB*, 99).[36] In one newspaper column he attacks lugubrious verse by panning *The Weeping Willow*, a Midwestern periodical that specialized in what Nye dubs "*post mortem poetry*." Nye calls the magazine "as depressing a sheet as one would crawl into at the Cockroach House, where we hired two warm rooms and slept in our overcoats and arctics." And he quotes one of the wretched death poems to illustrate what he calls "corduroy verse."[37] He made fun of poetry with uneven feet, saying of two poems he received in the mail from readers: "Every little while you find a line of size 9 with a D width, while the next one will have a C width and be much higher in the instep."[38]

Good original poetry, Nye realized, is especially difficult to write when one can so easily succumb to the temptation to imitate other poets. He advised one fledgling poet:

I would suggest that you make a bold dash for success by writing things that other people are not writing, thinking things that other people are not think-ing, and saying things that other people are not saying. . . . Who is writing the poetry that will live? Is it the man who is sawing out and sandpapering stanzas of the same general dimensions as some other poet? . . . Ah, No! . . . Show me the poet who is intimate with nature and who studies the little joys and sorrows of the poor; who smells the clover and writes about live, healthy people with ideas and appetites. He is my poet." ("To An Embyro Poet," *R*, 500–501)

Finally, Nye makes an appeal to the imaginative quality of poetry: "Poetry, like music, should inspire those who are capable of receiving inspiration, but it should not be too graphic, like the report of a United States coast survey."[39]

Nye used his newspaper columns during the New York years and afterward to comment on problems and conditions facing the writer. He was sympathetic with the outcry for a firm international copyright law,[40] sensitive to the perils of publishing—the way a writer could be mistreated by his publisher as well as by a hostile public[41]—and concerned over the conflict between social demands on an author and his need for privacy and tranquillity in which to write. He once complained that he could not meet all the social demands made upon him "without neglecting the literary work to which I have pledged my life, my fresh young intellect and my sacred honor."[42] Of course, writers bring some problems on themselves, Nye is quick to point out. He is disappointed that so many literary men are impractical: they should have a business head and sense of what is marketable. And they should be economical with words.[43]

Individual writers are often singled out for comment in Nye's columns. He praises, on the American side of the Atlantic, the poetry of his lecture partner, James Whitcomb Riley,[44] discusses the realistic tastes of William Dean Howells,[45] and touches on the nature and merits of Whitman's and Lowell's poetry, proclaiming the latter's *Biglow Papers* unreadable to a modern audience.[46] He compares the wit and humor of Oliver Wendell Holmes and Riley, seeing the former writer as given over to puns and conundrums, Riley to "practical" humor.[47] He writes character sketches of Eugene Field, Bret Harte, Joel Chandler Harris, and J. M. Bailey.[48] And he even devotes one clever article to kinds of writing instruments used by such literati as John Greenleaf Whittier, Riley, Mary Catherwood, Charles Dudley Warner, Rose Terry Cooke, R. H. Stoddard, and Mark Twain, giving a personal glimpse at each author in the process.[49]

Nye was impressed with the literary scene across the Atlantic, especially in London, but he was not always willing to praise. In a column written while he was in London he expresses amazement at the hearty lives and prolix productions of the Author's Club—such men as Walter Besant, Douglas Sladen, Gilbert Parker, and Conan Doyle. He marvels at their conditioning—how they grind out so many works; he is especially amazed by the energetic Dickens, who leads a dynamic life of prolific writing, heavy eating, and excessive walking. Nye cannot maintain the pace, personally or literarily, of these authors, and he is envious.[50]

Toward the works of Browning and Pope and the public readings of Edwin Arnold, however, Nye was uncomplimentary. Browning is a "fifteen-puzzle poet," an "over-estimated man. . . . His poetry reads like the chess column in a farm paper, and is more like a rebus than it is like the outpouring of a great, beautiful gob of passion." In short, Nye likes poetry "which does not call so much for brain fog as it does for the responsive sentiments in the human heart."[51] Nye's comment on Pope is not a particularly serious one and is not so negative as on Browning. During Nye's second sojourn in England in 1893 he wrote, "If he had not been snatched away before I came to England Pope and I would have helped each other. He was strong in some ways, while I came out better in others. Pope could have shown me how to get about London by the mysterious railroads, while I could have corrected his essays for him."[52] Nye's disappointment with poet Sir Edwin Arnold mainly involved Arnold's public readings, Nye claiming that the poet's inflections and gestures were poor.[53]

Dickens was the one nineteenth-century English author who caught Nye's fancy, and Nye could hardly praise him enough. He calls Dickens "my favorite author,"[54] and defends his reputation against the attack by William Dean Howells: "in fifty years from now let us ask the timid little touch-me-not who sells books on the train how William and Charles are standing as to sales of books."[55]

Nye's numerous articles and comments on the literary scene make it clear that though he sometimes enjoyed passing himself off publicly as a nonliterary man, he was actually much involved with the world of belles-lettres and empathized with the conditions and problems of the writer's world. Nye's claim that he was "a great bookworm and an omniverous reader"[56] is proved over and again by the literary interest evinced in his newspaper columns and published books—not just in his criticism but in his own creative pieces as well.

V   *His Books*

The New York years of 1887–1891 also resulted in several new Nye books. The bonanza year was 1888: in addition to *Nye and Riley's Railway Guide,* discussed in the preceding chapter, that year witnessed the publication of *Bill Nye's Chestnuts Old and New: Latest Gathering* and *Bill Nye's Thinks.*[57] Both books are essentially collections of Nye's newspaper columns or reprints from earlier books.

Chestnuts contains much material from *Bill Nye and Boomerang, Baled Hay,* and *Forty Liars,* but it has forty-four pieces that appear in book form for the first time. What Nye does with organization and

type of material included is one of the most redeeming aspects of the
book. The three parts are composed of "Chestnut-Burrs" (forty-six
essays, sketches, and narratives), "Poetic Chestnuts" (seven poems by
Nye), and "A Bushel of Smaller Chestnuts" (some fifty-eight brief
space fillers running in length from a few lines to several paragraphs).
Some of the "Smaller Chestnuts" are scattered throughout the volume
while others are grouped at the end. The book is illustrated by Frederick Opper, Livingston Hopkins, and one Williams.

There is nothing surprising or new about the "Chestnut Burrs," the
longer pieces Nye has collected. They consist of the usual assortment
of essays, anecdotes, and vignettes found in most of Nye's books. The
majority of them are favorite articles from previous publications plus
a smattering of more recent newspaper columns. Nye includes pieces
on such topics as the Shakespeare-Bacon puzzle, French masterpieces
at the Academy of Design, his attempt at writing a novel, female suffrage in Wyoming, and the Indians of the West. He reprints such
favorites as "A School of Journalism" and "The True Story of Damon
and Pythias." The poetry is distinguished only by the mock heroic
"Apostrophe To An Orphan Mule" and "Apostrophe Addressed To O.
Wilde." An introductory essay to Nye's "Poetic Chestnuts," "Nye as
Poet and Nye as Critic," is a spoof of himself as poet. Presenting himself in the third person, Nye writes, "A new and dazzling literary star
has rised above the horizon, and is just about to shoot athwart the starry
vault of poesy. How wisely are all things ordered, and how promptly
does the new star begin to beam, upon the decline of the old" (*C*,
258)—the "old" being the outrageous "Sweet Singer of Michigan,"
Julia A. Moore. Facetiously, Nye quotes lines of his poetry, then praises
them lavishly: "Ah! how true to nature and yet how grand. How broad
and sweeping. How melodious and yet how real. None but the true
poet would have thought to compare the close of life to the sudden
and unfortunate chuck of the off hind wheel of a lumber wagon into
a rut" (*C*, 259). Nye concludes,

If we could write poetry like that, do you think we would plod along the
dreary pathway of the journalist? Do you suppose that if we had the heaven-
born gift of song to such a degree, that we could take hold of the hearts of
millions and warble two or three little ditties like that, or write an elegy
before breakfast, or construct an ionic, anapestic twitter like the foregoing,
that we would carry in our own coal, and trim our own lamps, and wear a
shirt two weeks at a time? (*C*, 259–60)

It is actually the "Smaller Chestnuts," however, that add a slightly different flavor to this volume, for they are uncharacteristically aphoristic. Nye's lines may not be the sharply chiseled aphorisms of a Josh Billings, as pointed out in chapter 2, but the thoughts are as penetrating. On the transience of life, Nye writes, "Another landmark [the passing of a special day] has been left behind in our onward march toward the great hereafter. We come upon the earth, battle a little while with its joys and its griefs, and then we pass away to give place to other actors on the mighty stage" ("Sweet Saint Valentine," C, 273). On fame he writes: "A man works twenty years to become known as a scholar, a newspaper man and a gentleman, while the illiterate murderer springs into immediate notoriety in a day, and the widow of his victim cannot even get her life insurance. These things are what make people misanthropic and tenacious of their belief in a hell" ("Sudden Fame," C, 285). On gun control: "If revolvers could not be sold for less than $500 a piece, with a guarantee on the part of the vendee, signed by good sureties, that he would support the widows and orphans, you would see more longevity lying around loose, and Western cemeteries would cease to roll up such mighty majorities" ("How To Deal With The Revolver Difficulty," C, 248). On contending against invincible power:

We may often learn a valuable lesson from the stubborn mule, and guard against the too protuberant use of our own ideas in opposition to other powers against which it is useless to contend. It may be wrong for giant powder to blow the top of a man's head off without cause, but repeated contests have proved that even when giant powder is in the wrong, it is eventually victorious. ("A Lesson From The Mule," C, 251)

And on firmness:

Firmness is a good thing in its place, but we should early learn that to be firm, we need not stand up against a cyclone till our internal economy is blown into the tops of the neighboring trees. Moral courage is a good thing, but it is useless unless you have a liver to go along with it. Sometimes a man is required to lay down his life for his principles, but the cases where he is expected to lay down his digester on the altar of his belief, are comparatively seldom. ("Firmness," C, 257)

There are many other "Smaller Chestnuts" that express Nye's feelings on such varied topics as the English joke, the true marriage, and modern fiction. These pithy kernels of thought add spice to an otherwise conventional book of Nye's short prose pieces and poems.

The other major book of 1888 was *Bill Nye's Thinks*, subtitled *Prepared at the Instigation of the Author in Response to a Loud, Piercing and Popular Demand*. It was an inexpensive paperback designed to be sold to railway passengers. In his preface, "Premonitory Thinks," Nye acknowledges that some readers will feel he is lowering his literary standards by producing an inexpensive book, but he counters by asserting that prices of literature are lower now than a few centuries ago; even *Paradise Lost*, for which Milton received forty dollars, can be bought now for "as low as 25 cents" (*T*, 4). Besides, Nye quips, he "would rather disseminate five hundred thousand low-price books than to print a $27 book and have to read it myself" (*T*, 5).

Aside from the introductory address to the reader, almost all of the remaining twenty-eight selections are reprints of columns Nye had recently penned for the *World*. He writes spiritedly on his experiences in Washington, D.C., where he was sent on assignment by his paper, and reacts to the sights of New York, the countryside and climate of North Carolina, the design of the naval yard at Brooklyn, Indian affairs, and recent developments in politics and government, such as the farmers' problems with a high tariff. Other topics range from troubles with gardening and merits of rhubarb pie to the "desperate" straits of William H. Vanderbilt, whose fortune "has shrivelled down to $150,000,000" ("A Plea For One In Adversity," *T*, 143). He includes two of the "Dear Henry" letters to his son, an editorial praising the efforts of Cornell to found a school of journalism, and a satire on *Webster's Unabridged Dictionary*, depicting it as a badly written novel with "too many characters . . . at the expense of the plot" ("Webster And His Great Book," *T*, 177).

Though brief, *Thinks* is one of Nye's most successful books as far as enjoyable browsing is concerned—even for the modern reader. The reviewer for *The Book Buyer* pointed out long ago that the volume "contains some of the popular humorist's happiest hits,"[58] and *The Critic* felt that the selections would provide readers with "many an amused half-hour's reading."[59]

In the summer of 1890 Nye decided to write, illustrate, and publish *An Almanac For 1891*.[60] Comprising thirty-two pages—two of them advertising for the Rock Island Railway and the Equitable Life Assurance Society—the twenty-five-cent pamphlet had potential, but fell far short of being either a full-fledged serious almanac in the vein of Rob-

ert Bailey Thomas's *Old Farmer's Almanac* or a comic production
such as Henry Wheeler Shaw's *Josh Billings' Farmer's Allminax*. In
the strictest sense, it is not an almanac at all. The calendar pages are
mere monthly listings of days and dates with corresponding important
or bogus events alongside each date. Absent is all the usual apparatus
of the almanac. There are no tables of stages of the moon or positions
of the constellations, no weather calculations or editorial comments on
the meaning and behavioral implications of the astrological signs—
none of the fare Josh Billings handled with such rich burlesque in his
ten-year run of the *Allminax*.[61] Nye's lists of historical events are
largely serious and accurate, but enough of the comic is interspersed
to provide some light entertainment for readers bored by columns of
straight facts. For example, on Monday 16 March we are told that
"Abel adopted suspenders, B. C.," and Friday 20 March reads, "Uncle
Tom's Cabin co. eaten up by hogs" (*A*, 13). Monday 1 June shows
"Kentucky admitted after passing the breath tester with great difficulty, 1792" (*A*, 19), and Monday 6 July announces "Marriage of one
of Siamese twins; his brother greatly surprised, but concluded to be
present" (*A*, 21). Otherwise, the calendar pages are devoid of the special humorous devices that so enliven most burlesque almanacs.

Except for the humorous events dotting the calendar pages, the only
attempt to burlesque the almanac tradition is found at the beginning
of the booklet. Nye depicts the "Zodiac Man," his version of the Man
of the Signs, in disreputable state—scraggly beard, black eye, and
attempting to cover his nude body with newspaper pages. He is smoking a corncob pipe. Nye's accompanying admonition reads,

Very few of us, as we sit in our cosy homes by the bright warm fire, or
stroll gaily down Broadway, warmly clad and well, pause to think that on
these cold, bleak days, the Zodiac man must suffer a good deal. No one who
has ever tried it can realize what an effort it must require to pull one's self
together under such circumstances.

Then let us do all we can for him, wherever he may be, and resolve to put
something in his stocking if we can afford it. A Home for Disabled Zodiac
Men, where they could go and be treated occasionally, would be a good thing.

Who will be the first to move in this direction? (*A*, 3–4)

Finally, each left-hand page facing the calendar pages is filled with
Nye's comments on a wide variety of subjects. Some serious, some
humorous, these passages range from one-liners such as "Never look a
gift cottage in the gambrel roof" (*A*, 12) to an essay "On The Care Of

The Conscience" (A, 28–30). The comments are often more epigrammatic than most of Nye's statements, and they make interesting browsing. The only other distinctive feature of the *Almanac* is the clever illustrations that appear on many of the comments pages. Nye did them himself, and they attest to his ability with the comic drawing pen. Especially effective is one self-caricature, dubbed "The author in his study, in the act of thinking about the need of an Almanac for this year" (A, 4). It depicts a skinny, pensive Nye sitting at his desk in a dilapidated room, a diminutive hat perched on the top of his bulb-shaped head.

Nye published the almanac himself, having written the interested Major Pond on 31 August 1890, "I thank you for the generous offer for the almanac or an interest in it. I also have a similar offer from another quarter but shall publish myself I think and take the chances."[62] A later communication with the major implies that Nye thought of enlarging the project, perhaps extending his almanacking to other years, but he obviously decided against it. "As to the Almanac it is out of the question. With all else I have to do I have had to refuse barrels of work of the best and paying class, and with what I have agreed to do before can not add anymore."[63]

VI   Farewell to Gotham

Early in 1891 Nye decided to move his family from Staten Island back to his "Sunny Southern Home" in Asheville. He was tired of New York City and concerned about the effects of New York climate on his children's health, especially since his young son Ned had died there.[64] Before making the move, however, he arranged with Pulitzer for the continued publishing and even syndication of his Sunday columns, despite the fact Nye would be living away from New York City.[65]

The arrangement with the *World* continued satisfactorily until there was a shake-up in the newspaper front office in the late spring of 1891. Colonel John Cockerill, managing editor and Nye's close friend, decided to leave the *World* and purchase several newspaper companies of his own. Nye determined to go with Cockerill, switching his Sunday column from the *World* to the papers owned by his friend. Thus, the Sunday *World* for 14 June 1891 carries the last of Nye's regular contributions to Pulitzer's paper. The *World* tried to coax Nye back into its fold, but without immediate success.[66] Eventually, however, full exposure as a syndicated writer meant enjoying the wide circulation the *World* had to offer, and Nye decided in January 1891 to begin allowing the American Press Humorists Association, his syndicate, to distribute his letter through the *World* once again (though it never appeared as regularly as when Nye wrote directly for that paper). Ultimately, then, business took precedence over friendship.[67] Much was at stake, however, for Nye was now so popular that he was enjoying wide circulation both in America and England, and the American Press Humorists Association had formed ambitious plans for Nye's future, to the point of hoping to send him around the world at their expense.[68] To reap the benefits, Nye had to play the game.

CHAPTER 6

Tar Heel Man of Letters

THE North Carolina years, 1891–1896, were Nye's last but also his
most productive as far as quantity of output and variety of writings
are concerned. He wrote two successful books of comic history, a major
(and his last) book of essays and sketches, and an unpublished novel.
Moreover, he turned his attention to the theater, writing one successful
Broadway play and coauthoring a musical comedy which also played
on Broadway. All the while he continued to write his weekly syndicated newspaper columns and to lecture widely. These were years that
found Nye settled comfortably in his spacious Arden, North Carolina,
mountain home, Buck Shoals—that is, when he was not traveling as
newspaper correspondent or on the lecture circuit. They were also
years during which he suffered increasing spells of ill health, and his
ailments culminated in the fatal onset of disease early in 1896.

I Captivated by Carolina

Just as the New York period had its special influence on Nye's development, so the North Carolina sojourn affected his whole outlook and
the nature of his productivity for the last years. Many of his Sunday
columns express his interest and delight in his mountain environment.
Frequently he writes about the commodious house he built in 1891–
1892 on nearly one hundred acres of forest and farm land overlooking
the French Broad River near Asheville. He was exceedingly proud of
the edifice and kept his readers informed on everything about it from
the new well dug with great difficulty to the fire that once broke out
and threatened the entire structure. In his rural retreat Nye expanded
his interests to include the flora and fauna of the area and the whole
subject of farming. He became quite a naturalist and staunch advocate
of rural western North Carolina, commenting on the ideal climate and
beautiful natural growth of the area, especially the variety of trees and
blooming shrubs and flowers. Nye decided he had located in the most

sylvan, bucolic area in the entire country. In a renewed spirit of enthusiasm for nature, he proclaimed in 1894, "I like nature. Give me plenty
of nature to commune with and a shag bark hickory tree against which
to agitate my back, and I am pleased as a child."[1] With such an enjoyable environment, he now found travel and winter sojourns elsewhere
harder to tolerate. As early as October 1891, having spent only one
summer in North Carolina, he complained, upon returning to New
York for a winter of work, that "rustic from the woods of North Carolina" finds himself "bewildered" by New York life, especially the
noise and confusion on Broadway. He christens himself "a pastoral person . . . interested in the growth of plant life. . . ."[2]

Nye's appetite for working the soil had been aroused in Wisconsin
and whetted in Laramie, Wyoming, where even with sharp winds and
frigid temperatures he had attempted to raise vegetables. Now, surrounded by his large estate, the temptations of farming were especially
alluring. Though he actually farmed on a relatively small scale, he soon
considered himself the seasoned farmer, often spicing his columns with
agricultural shop talk and showing sympathy for the plights of farmers.
He prescribed rules for farm work and good production[3] and defended
the farmer against President Grover Cleveland's accusation that the
American farmer made promiscuous use of certain seed products.[4] In
one column, he reminds his readers: "And to whom do we look with
more anxiety for our own weal than the farmer? Is he not the only
man who produces food sufficient for himself and others? We cannot
eat the wares of Mr. Tiffany nor yet the beautiful fabrics of Worth."[5]
After a year's residence in North Carolina, Nye bragged that he was
a farmer "by birth and natural selection," going so far as to claim,
"Literature with me has been merely a fad, an incident, as it were.
Farming has been my joy, my life, my boon, my outing, my vocation,
my dream and my religion."[6]

Rural life led Nye to delight in the various species of animals,
whether wild or domesticated. He was fascinated by the razorbacks of
the North Carolina woods,[7] wrote a humorous history of ornithology
and an essay on farm fowls,[8] celebrated the oyster,[9] and recounted his
personal lifetime ownership of dogs.[10] At the Chicago World's Fair he
was most impressed with the taxidermy exhibits.[11] And when he met
an authority on monkeys, in London in 1894, he devoted a whole column to what monkeys know and can do.[12] Kindness to animals became
a ruling passion with him. Reacting to the custom of docking horses'
tails, Nye fervently exhorts mankind to act charitably toward animals:

Let us, then, show signs of progress in the treatment of our dumb beasts. Read "Black Beauty" and buy it for your grooms. Remember that "the merciful man is merciful to his beast," and while you are using every faculty that God has given you to fight flies on these long summer days think of your poor, crippled horse beating his system with his maimed and mutilated tail.[13]

Nye took great pride in and gave special care to his matching, black, Kentucky-bred horses and two fine saddle horses,[14] and he thought enough of his milk cow, Fillay de Biff, to write a Sunday column on her when she died.[15] Even his duck Francis Drake and plough mule Juanita caught his fancy and received favored attention.[16] Indeed, Nye's last years in North Carolina saw him adopting a definite Thoreauvian view of his "brute neighbors."

II *Next Door to Wealth and Society*

Nye's Buck Shoals abutted George W. Vanderbilt II's Biltmore estate, the sprawling barony that occupied most of what is now Pisgah National Forest, south of Asheville. In 1891 and 1892, while Nye was building Buck Shoals and Vanderbilt was starting the Biltmore mansion, Nye frequently devoted portions of his columns to the proximity and relationship between himself and the commodore's grandson. As he did also in the case of Jay Gould, Nye feigned a bosom friendship that made him appear to be on intimate, neighborly terms with Vanderbilt. He put them both in the roles of ordinary, industrious farmers struggling to make a living out of the clay soil of western North Carolina. Share and share alike seemed to be the order of their friendship: "No man need ever ask for a better neighbor than George is. He helps me during the hoeing season and I help him in harvest. We own a thrashing machine together, and in the fall we not only do our own thrashing with it, but can make as high as $80, we think, by thrashing for the neighbors."[17]

Nye jested lightly about Biltmore's being adjacent to his land, claiming that he had his gardener construct a curb at the lower edge of his garden "to keep the potatoes from falling out of the ground and injuring Mr. Vanderbilt's cotton crop and pajama plants. . . ."[18] And he liked to look down on Vanderbilt's tennis court because it gave him "the benefit of the game without the fatigue of playing it."[19] When Nye's house was robbed, he surmised that the burglars must have thought the Nyes had borrowed the Vanderbilt's expensive plate to use for din-

ners.[20] The joking turned a bit sour, however, when Vanderbilt began
buying land all around Buck Shoals. Nye grew defensive, declaring he
would not sell to Vanderbilt even if he were surrounded and pressured.
"But I will not yield. I am like a colored man whose little farm still
stands in the center of Mr. Vanderbilt's first purchase and who refuses
to sell for 1,000 times the value of his little place."[21] Shortly after 1892,
comments on Vanderbilt largely disappear from Nye's writings, perhaps in part because of the extended absences of both landowners from
their respective estates as well as Nye's loss of enthusiasm for his rich
neighbor when the Vanderbilt empire began to threaten strangulation.

The city of Asheville, ten miles north of Buck Shoals, caught Nye's
interest and sometimes his derision, as it would Thomas Wolfe's in the
next few decades. In a satiric article that seems to anticipate Wolfe's
ridicule of the society columns in the *Raleigh News and Observer* (in
Look Homeward, Angel) Nye gives local socialites such absurd names
as Pearl Pffooffer, Recompense Stillwagon, Phoebe Beebe, and Pre-
cious Idea Wipes.[22] Overall, Nye's appraisal of his neighbors was
mixed. He was somewhat proud to live "next door" to Vanderbilt, and
he admired the enterprising nature of the Asheville denizens, but he
felt threatened by the former and was critical of the shallow social
values of the latter.

With the rural people of the area, however, Nye was understanding
and congenial. Toward the Negro he was not totally above condescen-
sion; yet, considering his harsh views of Indians and Mormons, his
attitude was sometimes surprisingly tolerant—sometimes even supportive. He was proud that Southern cities, with their preponderance
of black workers, did not have the strikes and other labor problems of
Northern cities where hardly any Negroes lived. And he envisioned a
bright future for the black worker in an emerging industrial South:
"The colored man will yet prove no doubt a blessing when new indus-
tries open up in the South, and with his wonderful powers of imitation
and quickness to learn all sorts of manual work he is most assuredly a
safer man to employ, if he could have the training, than a fire-eating,
disturbing, dynamiting outcast from Europe."[23] Nye called for philan-
thropists such as Carnegie and Gould to start a school to train young
blacks for trades, "so that a peaceful but dependent race might have
a job," believing such a move would "be a great and good work
applauded by God and humanity."[24] Once ordered out of a railroad
car reserved for blacks, Nye reacted indignantly since, he declares, his
ancestors fought for emancipation of the slaves and he himself had

tried to help the race whenever he could. He concludes, "Race prejudice is an awful thing. . . . Race prejudice is a thing I hate. I have never
missed an opportunity to elevate the colored race whenever I
could. . . ."[25]

Nye's attitude toward the black paralleled his whole new perspective
of the South. He saw much to admire and yet much growth and progress yet to be experienced. He liked the orderly life of the South, being
enough of an elitist to prefer social stratification in society (though he
still championed the rights and integrity of individuals of any class). In
all, the South and its people—black and white—offered a pleasant
ambiance; and Nye's newspaper columns postmarked "Buck Shoals,
Arden, N.C." reflect his delight in being there.

III   *Peripatetic Nye: London, Washington, Nassau*

Much as Buck Shoals and western North Carolina held Nye's affec-
tion, he was still called forth to make a living. And although he now
could write his weekly columns at home, he still had to move about in
the world in order not to grow stale as a viable commentator. In addition, his lecture travels and the writing and production of two plays
for Broadway required that he be away from Buck Shoals for lengthy
periods. In the five years before his death, he spent parts of two
autumns in New York and one fall and winter in Washington, D.C. He
attended the World's Fair in Chicago in 1893, and he made excursions
to England and the Bahamas. Most of these trips were sponsored by
the American Press Humorists Association, which was syndicating
Nye's weekly columns. His extensive travels and winter sojourns
shaped a substantial number of the columns he wrote for the newspapers during these final years of his life.

Nye's popularity abroad, won by his books and columns, prompted
numerous speaking invitations, and he responded with a London visit
in 1893. The fifteen London columns which appeared in syndicated
newspapers from 29 October 1893 to 14 February 1894 are among
Nye's liveliest writings. Traveling about town with his gourmandish
valet Clarence—who rivals some of Mark Twain's most colorful "Fer-
gusons" in *The Innocents Abroad*—Nye and his companion become
a veritable Don Quixote and Sancho, providing a roving picture of
London history, institutions, and current social life. Nye discusses art
museums, London literary circles, and special sites such as the Tower
of London, capturing the sense of history and the moods and rhythms

of the city. As mentioned in chapter 5, however, his main interest in the travel columns is always people,[26] even when he treats them satirically. In several of these 1893 London sketches he satirizes royalty with a flourish that rivals Mark Twain's treatments. A spurious interview with Prince Albert Edward has the royal son saying of his mother's long reign, "Of course I am as fond of Mother as anybody could be, but sometimes I think that both she and Bill Gladstone are running longevity into the ground."[27] In another column Nye writes of calling at Buckingham Palace, palette in hand, to ask if he may use the drawing room.[28]

One special reason Nye had gone to London was to appear at the 28 September dinner in honor of Emile Zola. Though Nye did not write a column on the dinner, it was an important occasion and a prestigious one for him, as he found himself at the same table with the guest of honor, Thomas Hardy, G. Du Maurier, Henry Arthur Jones, W. W. Astor, and Frank Harris.[29] In all, the London trip was one of Nye's most successful stays anywhere, and it brought to his writings a host of fresh topics of which his fertile imagination made the most. Nye's sense of the history of England is evident in several of his columns, the one for 19 November 1893,[30] for example, burlesquing the founding of London as well as other subjects he would deal with extensively in his full-length book on English history, to be discussed later.

Nye and his family spent the winter of 1894–1895 in Washington, D.C. Son Frank Nye later recalled the reasons behind the temporary move:

> Nye did not want to go stale. Rural life at Buck Shoals provided much good copy, but there was danger of monotony. Lecturing with its hardships provided change, stimulated new thoughts. There was to be no lecturing this winter. My sisters were in school in Washington, and as my father had always liked the capital and joyed to be close to the fountainhead of government, we took up our abode there in December.[31]

Nye had a marvelous stay in the capital. Frank Nye wrote that his father seemed delighted to be back in urban society after three years in the country and that he was excited by Washington's theaters, thriving commerce, and governmental activities. "Most of the time he was gay and sparkling."[32]

Interested in theater and commercialism he perhaps was, but the large majority of the nine columns postmarked "Washington, D.C."

concern government and politics, two of Nye's favorite subjects: "I like Washington, as we say in North Carolina, right much. I have had no leisure for loneliness or ennui. The man who can be ennuied in Washington must be an abnormal anthropoid. Here you see everybody. The people send their statesmen here, and then come here to see how they are behaving themselves. Thus we have the opportunity of meeting the eminent, and those who made them so."[33] As for meeting the "eminent," in his columns Nye fabricates a chatty meeting with Vice-President Adlai Stevenson aboard a passenger car,[34] describes meeting the president in the White House and attending a diplomatic reception there,[35] and details his familiarity with other governmental leaders. Grover Cleveland was in his second administration in this winter of 1894–1895, and, though Cleveland was a Democrat, Nye was generally supportive, backing the president on most issues except his treatment of farmers and his belief in a graduated income tax.

Beneath the glitter and excitement of Washington, however, Nye found much to criticize. On the light side, he wrote that since Washington people were faced with insufficient housing, someday the Washington Monument, Capitol dome, and George Washington's tomb would be converted to flats.[36] Commenting on the drab, clinical look of the White House, he averred there was not a New York policeman who did not have a "better shanty"; the rooms on the first floor of the executive mansion "look as cosy and homelike as the Brooklyn Bridge."[37] But most of his satire resulted from deeper concerns. Nye was especially alarmed over the inefficiency and inefficacy of government. He was chagrined that government was cumbersome in size, bogged down by bureaucracy, and impersonal and self-seeking. Whereas statesmen should be primarily concerned with issues and serving their constituents, they allow personal ambitions and the social whirl of Washington to take precedence. One of Nye's columns, fabricating an intimate conversation between himself and President Cleveland, reveals the president bemoaning his lack of control over and failure with an ill-behaved, recalcitrant Congress. The president complains to Nye: "'Formerly Congress used to come right up to me and look me straight in the eye and allow me to smell its breath, and there was absolute confidence between us, but now the moment I go up there and listen to the conversation both Houses go into executive session, and I have to go out and sit on the doorstep.'"[38]

The actions, or inactions, of Congress dumfounded Nye. Amused over the endless and vapid oratory on the Senate floor, where he thought he would hear major issues being decided, he proclaimed the banter good only for the entertainment of a wearied brain: "The Senate chamber is to me this winter a most restful and reposeful spot. I know of no place where one may go and secure better results if suffering from brain fog, resulting from mental strain."[39] As to the archaic, incoherent nature of a typical Senate floor speech, Nye reports, "Now and then a demagogue gets the floor long enough to make a speech on the late war, but he is always unpopular, even with his friends. He is generally a man with a speech that has been lying in his trunk for thirty years, and he trots it out here at a time when the people are begging on bended knee for relief. Could anything be more depressing than a belated speech on slavery at a time when 65,000,000 people are imploring Congress to relieve present distress!"[40] With a shrug of his shoulders, he finally concludes that the Senate floor has quite another purpose than the ostensible one:

I used to think it would be very embarrassing to make a speech in Congress, but it is not. I used to believe that the great mass of surging brain all about me at such a time would depress and scare me into silence and idiocy; but, on the contrary, the Congressman, as a matter of fact, has the whole room to himself. It is a good quiet place to go and practice in. One can there train his voice to fit the acoustics of a hall and fit himself for the lecture platform. Quite a number of men are doing it this winter.[41]

On specific political and governmental issues, Nye believed in "a high protective tariff theoretically,"[42] but he opposed the graduated federal income tax and the Monroe Doctrine, thus holding to a fairly staunch Republican point of view. He advised against the income tax on grounds that it discriminated against those who are successful in business: "When we get where we must tax enterprise and impose a fine upon business intelligence by taxing a laudable ambition and exempting and rewarding mismanagement we need the aid and commiseration of other nations. It is the praiseworthy ambition of every good citizen to make of his particular business an honorable success. The income tax punishes him for this. . . ."[43]

If Nye was disappointed in the workings of government, he nevertheless found politics a fascinating, if puzzling, game and Washington an exciting place. His winter sojourn there was an enlightening experience for a man who, by quirks of fate, perhaps barely missed being a professional politician himself.

Nye's last major excursion during the North Carolina years to receive major attention in his newspaper columns was the Bahamas venture in January and February of 1895. The trip, recorded in columns from 10–31 March 1895, was literally a disaster and almost proved fatal to Nye, as his ship hit a coral reef and sank near the Bahamas.

In the column for 10 March Nye recounts the frightful details of the shipwreck, describing actions of the passengers and crew, and telling about the anxious hours that beset them when it seemed there would not be enough rescue boats to save them all:

We had grown to know and to like each other very much in our four days' voyage, and to see those agonized faces turned toward us and the pale and horrified fathers and husbands on our deck forced to see their families go down [in life boats] within forty yards of us or be torn to pieces by the serrated edges of the reefs and their bodies given to the waiting sharks—that was the trying time with us. . . . [44]

Finally, all aboard were saved and taken to Harbor Island, where they recuperated overnight and then were taken to Nassau. It took Nye several days to recover from the shock of the wreck, but after he did he seems to have enjoyed Nassau, especially observing the natives and the animal and plant life on the island.

IV   Nye As Playwright

Nye's interest in writing fiction and poetry were complemented by his experiments in dramatic composition. During the North Carolina period he wrote at least two plays and possibly a third[45] and saw one of them attain success on Broadway. He had been interested in theater for many years, attending plays, reviewing dramatic productions, and to some extent even associating with actors and other theater people. When in Laramie, in the early days of his career, he was interested in the traveling and locally produced shows that were staged periodically in various makeshift halls before Laramie built "a handsome opera house" ("Anecdotes Of The Stage," *R*, 430). And while traveling the circuit in the West, he visited a Chinese theater in Marysville, California, to see what the Asian Americans were doing with the art. Every facet of the theater—from the ill-fitting false bald heads and whiskers donned by actors ("The Stage Bald-Head," *BH*, 147–48) to the

mechanical problems with scenery encountered by a traveling company in Laramie ("The Mimic Stage," *BH*, 240–45)—intrigued him
and evoked his witty, if often critical, comments. Nye once wrote after
viewing Henry Irving's play *King Arthur* and thoroughly enjoying the
evening of theater: "I felt again I was moving among my own set."[46]
Indeed, he did enjoy meeting and writing about actors, and he related
anecdotes about such major stars as Edwin Booth, Edwin Forrest, and
Joseph Jefferson.[47] If we can believe Nye, he was introduced to Booth
on Cape Cod and even offered to write a humorous insert for Booth's
Hamlet.[48]

Undoubtedly part of the attraction of the lecture platform to Nye
was its close kinship with the theater. Nye always considered himself
something of the actor when lecturing. He apparently did try amateur
play-acting though his efforts proved unsuccessful; once, for example,
as leading man, he forgot his lines in a crucial love scene and recited
a poem instead ("Billious Nye And The Amateur Stage," *NB*, 176–78).
In one of his last newspaper columns he answered a correspondent who
asked about his aspirations of becoming an actor: "You were misin-
formed about my ambitions to shine as a tragedian when young. I did
do a little amateur acting and once went to a neighboring town quietly—on rubbers, in fact—to act out on the stage but gave it up."[49] But
the interest was there, and it lingered.

Especially while living in New York but also at other times, Nye
occasionally wrote witty reviews of specific plays and also of ballet and
opera.[50] Among the plays that appealed to him most and kept his
reviewer's pen busy were *Uncle Tom's Cabin*, *Julius Caesar*, and
Hamlet, though there were numerous other well-known and minor
plays that he commented on in his newspaper columns, especially during the late 1880s and 1890s. In one article he panned the actor playing
the part of Uncle Tom;[51] while in others he noted without surprise the
high emotional impact the closing scenes of the "Tom Shows" had on
audiences.[52] A review of *Julius Caesar* playing in New York turned
into a comic biography of Caesar replete with anachronisms and cleverly distorted facts.[53] With *Hamlet* Nye turned more serious critic, cas-
tigating actor James Owen O'Connor for what Nye considered a frolicsome, inappropriate rendition of the character of Hamlet,[54] and
offering his amused reactions to an Edwin Booth & Co. version without
Elizabethan costumes.[55] Nye's reviews are funny and sometimes pre-
posterous, but they are based on solid critical principles of dramatic
decorum and propriety.

With his combined interests in acting, attending productions, and associating with theater people, it is not surprising that Nye took the next step and tried writing his own plays. Most unfortunately, none of the plays he wrote are extant, with one possible exception,[56] and thus a discussion of Nye as playwright must rely on reviews and external source materials about his plays.

His career as a dramatist began in 1886 with two plays, *Gas Fixtures*, coauthored with playwright Scott Marble, and *The Village Postmaster*. The former was the result of Marble's writing Nye and proposing the joint authorship. When Nye responded, he seriocomically expressed his enthusiasm, his questions, and his doubts:

I have just received your favor of yesterday, in which you ask me to unite with you in the construction of a new play.

This idea has been suggested to me before, but not in such a way as to inaugurate the serious thought which your letter has stirred up in my seething mass of mind.

I would like very much to unite with you in the erection of such a dramatic structure that people would cheerfully come to this country from Europe, and board with us for months in order to see this play every night. . . .

Would you mind telling me . . . how you write a play? You have been in the business before, and you could tell me, of course, some of the salient points about it. Do you write it with a typewriter, or do you dictate your thoughts to someone who does not resent being dictated to?

Do you write a play and then dramatize it, or do you write the drama and then play on it? Would it not be a very good idea to secure a plot that would cost very little, and then put the kibosh on it, or would you put up the lines first, and then hang the plot or drama, or whatever it is, on the lines? Is it absolutely necessary to have a prologue? If so, what is a prologue? Is it like a catalogue? . . .

But seriously, a play, it seems to me, should embody an idea. Am I correct in that theory or not? It ought to convey some great thought, some maxim or aphorism, or some such thing as that. ("A New Play," *R*, 412–13)

Gas Fixtures was copyrighted in Chicago in 1886 by Nye, Marble, and producer Tony Denier.[57] Nye referred to his involvement in the play and its imminent production in a letter to Riley dated 14 April 1886:

"I have been squirting a few desultory remarks into the play of which I told you, and attending rehearsals. I will witness its first production on the traditional dog stage at Rochelle, Ill. After that I will go home and leave the

company on the road under the management of Tony Denier, who puts up
the funds and pays me a royalty. If successful the play will add considerably
to my great wealth."[58]

Unfortunately, we know little about its subject matter or its success.

The Villiage Postmaster, an autobiographical play based on Nye's
career as postmaster, justice of the peace, and editor in Laramie,
brought him little fame until it was rewritten in 1891—at actor friend
Stuart Robson's urging—as The Cadi.[59] The play opened on Broadway
at the Union Square Theater on 21 September 1891 and enjoyed 125
performances over the next three months, closing in New York on 19
December and then going on the road.

Again, there is no manuscript or printed version,[60] but newspaper
accounts and surviving advertisements of The Cadi reveal that the
play was a three-act comedy, the first two acts being set in Wyoming,
the third in New York.[61] The main character, the Cadi, was a Nye
persona, and the role was played by the famous actor Thomas Q. Seabrooke. There was some music in the production, for one song, "The
Prodigal Son," written by Nye for Seabrooke to sing, survives intact.[62]
The reviews of the play as drama—even comic drama—were mixed,
though more often harsh. The New York Times called it "not . . . a
play at all or a comedy at all, but simply three of Mr. Nye's Sunday
articles strung together and recited in costume by Mr. Thomas Q. Seabrooke," and judged it "an attempt to write a play which failed
because a series of jokes, no matter how good they may be, will not
take the place of actions and 'situations.'"[63] The personality of Bill Nye
was apparently the main attraction of the play, and that image was
attractive enough to compensate for the lack of action and cohesive
plot, at least as far as most theatergoers were concerned. Near the end
of The Cadi's run, the New York World remarked on its obvious success as a production, predicted a profitable road engagement following
its New York closing, and concluded, " . . . after all there is something
in the homely scenes and humor of the play and the long dryly comical
soliloquies of the chief actor that is exactly suited to the bucolic taste.
It is the very essence of Bill Nye boiled down, and Bill Nye with his
quaint forms of speech and mental absurdities is to the average American citizen the beau-ideal of humorists."[64] Further proof that Nye's
presence—as prototype for the lead—caused the play's success lies in
a story that was published in the World the morning after the play
closed. It seems that actor Seabrooke had been so certain he himself

was the main attraction that he insisted to the manager that his (Sea-brooke's) name be carried in larger print than Nye's on the marquee and playbills. But when Seabrooke withdrew toward the end of the run because of a badly sprained ankle and a minor actor took his part, "the audiences were as large and laughed as heartily as ever at the jokes of Mr. Nye; and Mr. Floyd [manager George W. Floyd] was convinced . . . that the author, after all, amounted to a little more than the actor."[65]

As an overall production, then, *The Cadi* was certainly a success, though it was weak as drama. Nye worried when some critics said the play dragged and the humor wore thin toward the end,[66] and he altered the script, improving the tempo and sharpening the repartee.[67] But he need not have worried about general audience reception, because his highly popular image, as portrayed in the title role, carried the play.

Nye's next dramatic endeavor, *The Stag Party*, was not successful at all. Coauthored with dramatist Paul Meredith Potter in 1895, the play was advertised as "musical travesty in three acts" and was staged at the Garden Theater in New York for twelve performances in December 1895.[68] Feeling that a large part of *The Cadi*'s failure as drama was due to the singular emphasis on the title character, Potter and Nye took pains to rid *The Stag Party* of the Nye personality and to emphasize a variety of characters. Nye provided song lyrics and humorous situations, but Potter was mainly in charge of the dramatic structure. The *New York Times* announced the day before the play opened, "It occurred to Mr. Potter that something novel could be done with what are practically old methods, and that each man and woman in the chorus could be made, in a certain sense, as important as a prin-cipal and a factor toward success."[69] The drama is set in the Adiron-dacks and satirically treats the sport of hunting. The protagonist, the attorney general of New York, supposedly shoots a guide rather than the stag he was pursuing, becomes a fugitive from justice, then discov-ers at the end of the play that the guide was not wounded at all, and the conflict is happily resolved.[70] The cast of characters included nobody famous but was large, and the production had an abundance of elaborate costumes, showy scenes, and dancing and singing.[71]

The reviews generally panned the production. Though giving credit to Nye's humorous touches and Potter's ambitious staging, the *Times* declared that "the combination of humorist and playwright has pro-duced nothing valuable"[72] and added,

There are two good comic songs, a funny darky and bear act, and a capital bit of travesty of romantic melodrama. All these things could be compressed into half an hour. To offset these there are two hours of pointless drivel, vulgarity, and cheap characterless music.

Fine scenery and dresses, a host of pretty girls, and one or two clever comedians are hopelessly wasted on "A Stag Party." They say at the Garden Theater that it is to be changed, revised, built-up, and made to go. Better make it a new piece.[73]

Another *Times* reviewer sighed, "But, alas! We expected better work from Paul Potter and Edgar Nye. They prove inferior to the ordinary London librettists. All that paint and powder, silk tights and lace petticoats, limelights, and scenery can do for 'A Stag Party' has been done. It may have a long run. But the Brooklyn Bridge may fall."[74] The *New York World*, Nye's sometime employer, looked forward to *The Stag Party* with enthusiasm, having heard of its being "a clever and amusing satire on some American peculiarities, worked out on highly original lines," and surmised, "'A Stag Party' ought to prove a very successful experiment."[75] But the opening night review, entitled "It Proved A Very Flat Stag Party," was wholly negative. In the *World's* opinion, "There was something inexpressibly sad about the production of 'A Stag Party' last night at the Garden Theater. What was designed to give pleasure to the public proved a most dreary and futile attempt. The audience was large and disposed to be kindly. It came there to assist at a success. It participated in a positive failure."[76] The *World* lamented that the "accomplished" Nye and Potter could produce "so meaningless and witless a piece as 'A Stag Party,'" especially since Nye is "the humorist who has given such enjoyment to millions of readers." Much like the *Times*, it concluded, "If there is any hope for 'A Stag Party' it will have to be completely rewritten. It would seem to be useless to attempt to doctor up its present story. All the tonics in the world could not invest it with vitality."[77]

Nye, of course, was extremely disappointed over the failure of the play, having written his mother before it was staged, "Of course I am very anxious about it, and should it succeed I'll have to go at another in January."[78] He was not wholly crushed by its failure, however; in fact, he reacted philosophically, again writing his mother on 6 January 1896: "I suppose I told you of the play? It is in the scrap pile after a very sad career of two weeks. However, we cannot always hit it. Some of the children of the brain are liable to be Gill Withams or Fred Swartouts."[79]

Though the issue is difficult to judge in the absence of a text it seems likely that Potter and Nye's conscious attempt to rid the play of the Nye persona and personality was ironically the reason for its failure. *The Cadi* had prospered despite its dramatic shortcomings because at least the audience was given Bill Nye. But *The Stag Party* was straight melodramatic spectacle, suffering from the lack of his personality as a major attraction and unifying factor.

V *Historical Burlesques*

Nye's two burlesques of history written in the 1890s were a natural culmination of his satirical leanings and his keen interest in historical personages and events. Brief biographies of historical personages appear throughout his works, though they increase in the late years as if Nye were consciously leading up to the writing of these two volumes. Walter Blair points out that in Nye's *Remarks* fourteen of the thirty-four burlesques deal with "famous warriors, emperors, or politicians of the past."[80] Nye writes on Franklin, John Adams, Columbus, George Washington, Mark Antony, Nero, Spartacus, George III, Plato, and Daniel Webster, among others. Other biographies appear in his newspaper columns of the late period. He often dwells on historical place and incident along with biography. In *Remarks* he includes a humorous history of Babylon plus accounts of Bunker Hill, the Old South Meeting Hall in Boston, and Boston Commons and environs. In his newspaper columns he gives burlesque historical accounts of Jerusalem and Plymouth Rock, among other places.[81] In all such writings, as Blair has observed, Nye's stance is that of the realist.[82] He views history with comic-critical analysis and appraisal, and he likes to introduce unglamorous, trivial detail in his accounts to de-emphasize the romantic and imaginative associations which usually accompany a view of the historical past.

Bill Nye's History of the United States appeared in 1894. Containing thirty-one chapters, a preface, and a one-page appendix, the work spans American history from the discovery of America by Columbus to the second presidential administration of Grover Cleveland.

The preface, coauthored by Nye and his illustrator Frederick B. Opper, dwells on the reason for the volume. Facts are the indisputable "framework of history," the two men admit, but need not be delivered to the reader bare: "We want to see them embellished and beautified. That is why the history is written."[83] Thus, the two vow to dress historical truths "in the sweet persuasive language of the author, and fluted, embossed, embroidered, and embellished by the skilful hand of the artist . . . " (*US*, 6). Nye and Opper view the role of history as "but the record of the public and official acts of human beings. It is our object, therefore, to humanize our history and deal with people past and present" (*US*, 6–7).

To "humanize" and "deal with people past and present" are indeed the watchwords of this history. Throughout Nye adheres to his announced purpose and sticks close to historical fact; at the same time, he embellishes the historical record with liberal interpretations, supposed motives and outcomes, and imaginative situations. He obviously knows his history—his facts are surprisingly accurate, and he has researched particulars to support any generalizations. At times, in fact, he becomes so caught up in the history or biography of a certain age or man that he forgets to be humorous and writes straight history. This habit is especially evident in the chapters on the Civil War.

One of the major themes of the book is the superiority of democracy over monarchy or any form of oppression. Except for his obvious prejudice against the American Indian, which still obtains even in this late book, Nye is strongly democratic and intolerant of groups or people who inhibited the growth of democracy in early America. It is quite clear in the early chapters on America's suppression by England and on the Revolutionary War that Nye is a fervent believer in individual sovereignty and liberty. Monarchy is the hated oppressor that repeatedly catches his ire. He is equally harsh on the Puritans because of their intolerance of other beliefs and ways and their cruelty to offenders. He charges that their involvement in witch persecutions proves that their "gospel privileges had not given their charity and Christian love such a boon as they should have done" (*US*, 59). He obviously admires Roger Williams and Anne Hutchinson for their rebellion against the Puritans and their dedication to religious liberty (chapters 4 and 5). On the whole matter of political and religious freedom and individual sovereignty, Nye admonishes, "Instead of turning over our consciences to the safety deposit company of a great political party or religious organization and taking the key in our pocket, let us have individual charge of this useful little instrument and be able finally to answer for its growth and decay" (*US*, 70).

The most profound and engaging section of Nye's history is the five chapters on the Civil War (chapters 24–28). Here he writes with vigorous intensity, high seriousness, and deftness of detail. Nye was obviously extremely interested in the Civil War era. In surprising detail he describes major and obscure battles and generals. On the war as a whole, he philosophizes that it was as unavoidable as the flood and as "idiotic in its incipiency as Adam's justly celebrated defense in the great 'Apple Sass Case.' ... Men will fight until it is educated out of them" (*US*, 250). But that inclination toward fighting is a rueful one, he is quick to add. Nye emerges in the *History* as a strong Unionist and pacifist-humanist, holding the Lincolnian view that the Union must be preserved and that the South must be forgiven and generously embraced by the North. On the Union, he asserts, "Let us be contented during this generation with the assurance that geographically the Union has been preserved, and that each contending warrior has once more taken up the peaceful struggle for bettering and beautifying the home so bravely fought for" (*US*, 304). Considering the South's part in the affray, Nye refers to the burning of Atlanta as "one of the saddest features of the war" (*US*, 286–87) and extolls the Southern soldier, "a beautiful gathering of foemen in whose veins there flowed the same blood as in their [the Union troops] own, and whose ancestors had stood shoulder to shoulder with their own in a hundred battles for freedom" (*US*, 281). And on Lincoln's assassination and the pangs of Reconstruction Nye observed: "It is very likely that the assassination of Lincoln was the most unfortunate thing that happened to the Southern States. While he was not a warrior, he was a statesman, and no gentler hand or more willing brain could have entered with enthusiasm into the adjustment of chaotic conditions, than his" (*US*, 308).

Again, it is surprising and illuminating that Nye devotes so much— over a sixth—of the *History* to the Civil War and that he is so detailed and so essentially serious. There is little humor and burlesque in the war section. Perhaps for Nye—avid Lincolnian Unionist and yet Southern sympathizer—the war had too many serious implications and was too recent a blight on the growth of America to be spoofed. He concludes the unit on the war with the statement, "we cheerfully close the sorrowful pages in which we have confessed that, with all our greatness as a nation, we could not stay the tide of war" (*US*, 296).

But, despite interludes of serious writing, the overall tone and style of the *History* are often humorous. Nye frequently dresses historical fact in witty expression and catchy phrase. For example, as Columbus prepares to set sail for the voyage on which he would find America, Queen Isabella brings him flowers and Ferdinand presents him with "a nice yachting-cap and a spicy French novel to read on the road"

(*US*, 19). When Roger Williams defects from the Puritans, he takes refuge among the Indians, finding them "open on Sundays" (*US*, 52). In anticipation of the arrival of Captain John Smith, Pocahontas and her father rehearse their feigned beheading act for a month, with her father acting as villain and Smith's part being played by a chunk of wood; thus, "they succeeded in getting their little curtain-raiser to perfection" (*US*, 38). During the Revolutionary War a cannonball roars through General Burgoyne's tent, knocking the pen from his hand. Nye understates, "Almost at once he decided to surrender" (*US*, 176). And on the election of Lincoln, he quips, "Lincoln was elected, which reminded him of an anecdote" (*US*, 246). There are numerous asides calculated to denigrate the Indians, English monarchs, or the Puritans, such as the last being described as landing at Plymouth during a storm and "noting the excellent opportunity for future misery, [beginning] to erect a number of rude cabins" (*US*, 47).

Several techniques in the book are specifically designed to burlesque historical or scholarly writing. Spurious bibliographies bearing inane or pun-ridden citations appear at the ends of some chapters. At the close of chapter 2, for example, Nye includes in his list of references, "*Why I Am An Indian*. by S. Bull. With Notes by Ole Bull and Introduction by John Bull" (*US*, 34). The reference note to chapter 6 includes the titles "*How to Keep Well*, by Methuselah, *Humor of Early Days*, by Noah, and *General Peacefulness and Repose of the Dead Indian*, by General Nelson A. Miles" (*US*, 70). Chapter 9 concludes with a list of examination questions with ridiculous answers. And many times throughout the text Nye inserts the parenthetical phrase "(see appendix)" after a particular statement, the joke being that when the reader turns to the appendix he finds only this short explanation:

> The idea of an appendix to this work was suggested by a relative, who promised to prepare it, but who has been detained now for over a year in one of the public buildings of Colorado on the trumped-up charge of horse-stealing. The very fact that he was not at once hanged shows that the charge was not fully sustained, and that the horse was very likely of little value. THE AUTHOR. (*US*, 329)

Thus scholarly apparatus of several different sorts is ridiculed in the *History*. Furthermore, Opper's copious drawings, though somewhat sketchy in quality, enhance the burlesque nature of the work by illustrating Nye's humorous observations and often caricaturing Nye himself.

On the whole, *Bill Nye's History of the United States* boasts some of Nye's best writing. His talents in description, narration, and analysis are perhaps more evident in their sustained effectiveness in this volume than in any other of his books. The style is almost always lively, witty, and smooth. The pages exude Nye's enthusiasm for history and register his delight in commenting caustically on its basic facts and cast of characters. Finally, the serious side of the volume vies with the humorous for precedence, as Nye found himself so taken by history that at times he forgot to be funny.

The book was published by J. B. Lippincott who recounts that with each batch of copy Nye included a humorous letter, parts of which overshadowed the humor in the historical chapter.[84] When Lippincott was disappointed with the first chapter and told Nye so, Nye wrote back, "'You must not shock my inspiration, for inspiration is a tender plant, requiring careful watering and bringing into the house of nights.'"[85] Lippincott abided by and learned from Nye's warning and left him alone for the duration of the writing. The results were most pleasing to author and publisher alike, for the book enjoyed eight printings the first year and sold at least 500,000 copies in all.[86] Nye, in a mood of elation and relief, wrote former lecture manager Major Pond in June 1894, "I'm glad you like the History. It is selling tip top and I am not going on the road [to lecture] in 95."[87] Substantial earnings from a single book had been a goal of Nye's for many years. He had finally met with that success from his first burlesque history.

So successful was the *History* that Nye and Lippincott were mutually enthusiastic about the prospects of a companion volume.[88] Thus, in 1895 Nye began writing *Bill Nye's History of England,* a volume that begins with the early Britons before Roman times and was to end in Nye's own century. But Nye's last illness and untimely death occurred while the book was still in progress. As publisher Lippincott recalled the situation,

When Nye commenced the *History of England,* the disease which finally carried him off was beginning to tell on him. Copy came slowly, and finally stopped. I had no idea he was so ill. I thought and hoped it was a temporary sickness. But about two weeks after I received chapter 18 of the *History of England* I read the news of the death of a man I loved, admired, and respected.[89]

Thus, as posthumously published in 1896, the book covers English history, to quote its subtitle, "From The Druids to the Reign of Henry

VIII." The narrative ends with a treatment of the Henry-Cardinal
Woolsey relationship, stopping just short of the entrance of Anne Bol-
eyn into Henry's life. The brief preface, written by the publisher,
acknowledges Nye's death and asserts that the unfinished book is in
Nye's best vein and is, typically, "not only amusing, but instructive as
well."[90] The editors stress that the dates and events are correct, though
embellished by Nye's "fancy," and "the leading historical characters
are made to play in fantastic *rôles*" (*E*, 5). Nye's serious vein is under-
scored as well: "Underneath all, however, a shrewd knowledge of
human nature is betrayed, which unmasks motives and reveals the true
inwardness of men and events with a humorous fidelity" (*E*, 5).

Nye's view of English history is anything but sanguine. The eighteen
chapters emphasize the barbaric nature and chaotic times of the early
inhabitants and settlers and reflect the deplorable antics of the monarchs throughout the history of the realm. The founders of England,
especially the Saxons, are portrayed as drunken ne'er-do-wells, who
were "marked by an eternal combat between malignant alcoholism
and trichinosis. Many a Saxon would have filled a drunkard's grave,
but wabbled so in his gait that he walked past it and missed it" (*E*, 30–
31). The Middle Ages and early Renaissance fare little better in Nye's
account, and very few monarchs from any period win any praise from
him at all. From the jealous Henry II to the "egotistical usurper" Richard III, Nye depicts English monarchs generally as immature, petty,
irresponsible, selfish, and quarrelsome. There are exceptions, notably
Alfred the Great, whom Nye considered a well-educated, studious man
and an effective leader. He lauds Alfred as "a brave soldier, a successful all-around monarch, and a progressive citizen in an age of beastly
ignorance, crime, superstition, self-indulgence, and pathetic stupidity"
(*E*, 48). Nye's quarrel with monarchy undoubtedly stems largely from
his democratic prejudice against the institution of rule by one. But he
finds throughout English history such political and governmental tur-
bulence that even his assessment of the democratic arm of English government, the House of Commons, is not especially favorable. With typical sarcasm he remarks, "The House of Commons is regarded as the
bulwark of civil and political liberty, and when under good police reg-
ulations is still a great boon" (*E*, 130).

Nye deplores especially the absence of an inclination toward learning among the early English people. One reason he praises Alfred is
that he was a king who actively tried to improve education. In origi-
nating the idea of bringing foreign scholars to Oxford University to

expose the students to alien cultures and orientations, Alfred was attempting to overcome "the hide-bound and stupid conservatism and ignorance bequeathed by father to son, as a result of blind and offensive pride, which is sometimes called patriotism" (*E*, 49). Of all the developments in English history, Nye singles out printing as the "most valuable" because "from this art came the most powerful and implacable enemy to ignorance and its attendant crimes that Progress can call its own" (*E*, 173). At least there was a modicum of attention paid to learning by the early English, just enough—Nye would say—to save them from total chaos and extinction as a nationality.

On the whole, Nye's *History of England* is not as humorous as the *History of the United States*. Absent are the burlesque devices such as mock bibliographical references and such comical pedantic asides as "(see appendix)." Even the use of comic techniques of understatement and anticlimax are few. What humor is present lies mainly in Nye's lively wit in phrasing his observations, narrations, and descriptions, and in exaggerating events outlandishly. Thus throughout the book there is constant interplay and effective tension between serious events and Nye's comic, often sardonic, reactions to those deeds and facts. The tone is not nearly as light as in most of the *History of the United States*. In fact, this comic-critical history is ultimately more "critical" than "comic."

While Nye was ill and unable to work on the *History of England*, illustrator W. M. Goodes kept busy with drawings that he felt would be needed eventually. Those drawings are grouped at the end of the text, the publishers announcing in an appendix that readers should appreciate the illustrations since they "have merit and humor of their own, independently of the text" (*E*, 195). Thus, some eighteen pages of drawings, covering English history from the time of Henry VIII to the reign of William and Mary, close out Nye's unfinished history of England, the only book he left incomplete at his death.

VI *Nye's Last Books*

As mentioned earlier, Nye's writings are so filled with anecdotes, dramatic situations, and character sketches that he seemed ready made for writing fiction. Many of his short pieces are essentially outlines for short stories or even novels. Though Nye once disclaimed any ambition of writing a novel, jesting, "I always thought it required more of a mashed raspberry imagination than I could muster" ("Bill Nye Essays

A Novelette," *C*, 170), in actuality he did make the attempt. Perhaps as a calisthenic preparation for a novel entirely of his own, he wrote the last chapter of a composite novel, *His Fleeting Ideal: A Romance of Baffled Hypnotism*, published by J. S. Ogilvie in 1890.[91] A melodrama of intrigue and adventure complete with pretty heroine, pompous hero, and a villain hypnotist, Nye's concluding chapter solves several dilemmas by means of a timely two-train collision and ties together all loose plot threads. His usual dry, sardonic wit prevails, making his chapter the most poignant, satiric, and enjoyable of all.

Nye's appetite for writing fiction was certainly whetted by this novel and the many vignettes he had written, but unfortunately these experiments never led to a published novel entirely of his own authorship. He came close, however, for he had the manuscript of a novel, "Thelma," with him on the near-tragic voyage to the Bahamas early in 1895. Unfortunately, "Thelma" was one of the possessions he was unable to retrieve from the sinking *Cienfuegas*.[92] There is no indication in any of Nye's comments as to the subject matter, theme, or type of novel he was attempting in "Thelma"; nor is there any indication that he thought of rewriting it after losing the manuscript. Thus Nye as novelist is, unfortunately, a closed subject. While there is little doubt that he could have drawn vivid characters and handled plot and action with aplomb, the lingering question, given the nature of his usual method and tone, is whether he could ever have achieved sufficient artistic distance to write a successful novel. It is likely that his accustomed authorial presence and sardonic commentary would have interfered with an effective presentation of his story, unless, of course, the tone of the book allowed for a familiar comic narrator in the vein of Fielding.

Within a few months of his loss of "Thelma," Nye did prepare another book for publication—the last collection of essays and sketches that he personally sanctioned and sent off to be published, *A Guest at the Ludlow*.[93] He died while the book was in press, and the publisher sought help from Nye's wife for financial arrangements and assistance from James Whitcomb Riley in reading the proof. Riley undertook the laborious task as a kind of testimonial to his late friend.[94] *Ludlow* appeared in 1896 and enjoyed favorable reception from public and critics alike, the *Overland Monthly*, for instance, proclaiming in characteristic praise: "The witless vulgarisms of many humorists have never had a portion in the work of Bill Nye, and this book throughout, overflows with the clean, good-natured jokes of America's great humorous writer."[95]

The majority of the twenty-eight essays and sketches in *Ludlow* are
reprinted from Nye's Sunday columns in the *New York World* and
other syndicated newspapers. Several, however, appear to have been
newly written or at least retouched if printed earlier.[96] As might be
expected in this late collection, the range of subjects is wide, the contents reflecting Nye's interests and his numerous spheres of habitation.
The variety of topics and richness of his late writing make the book
one of his most enjoyable for the modern reader.

In the lead sketch, from which the book gets its title, Nye cleverly
describes the Ludlow Street jail in New York City as if it were a Spar-
tan-like hotel and he was a guest there. He jests at the two ways of
gaining admittance to the jail: "You can pay five cents to the Elevated
Railroad and get here, or you can put some other man's nickel in your
own slot and come here with an attendant" (*L*, 2). Everything from
"registering" at the Ludlow ("[the clerk] does not seem to care whether
you have any baggage or not" [*L*, 5]) to examining the physical
appointments ("Heavy iron bars keep the mosquitoes out" [*L*, 6]) is on
the receiving end of Nye's witty commentary. He describes the different social classes present and charts their respective behavior. Ludlow
jail harbored both actual prisoners and occasional boarders, and Nye
contrasts the poor man who sleeps "in a stone niche near the roof" with
the boarder sporting good clothes, cigars, and brandy. The meals of
bread and soup cause Nye as much anguish as anything, since he is
something of a gourmet. By the time he has thoroughly scrutinized the
Ludlow jail, Nye has convinced the reader of his sense of relief that he
is only a temporary boarder and can soon leave the premises.

Ludlow contains sketches on other facets of life in New York (Central Park, Broadway traffic), essays on Nye's travels West—including
accounts of his real estate ventures there—humorous biographies of
Thomas Jefferson and Galileo, a piece on a mountain climb and discovery of an Indian legend in the Catskill Mountains, a seriocomic
review of a production of *Hamlet*, accounts of raising chickens and
running for public office, a vignette on eccentric summer boarders in
a rural North Carolina home, a projection on what life will be like in
the future, an admonition to prospective presidents to choose their
birth cottages with care (in the manner of Lincoln and Jackson), and
several other essays of personal reflections and philosophy.

Nye's remarks on politics, the growth and change of American life,
religion, and New York as microcosm of human types are particularly
memorable reflections in *Ludlow*. "As A Candidate" recounts his
unsuccessful campaign for the Wyoming legislature in 1877 and pre-

sents some of Nye's most cynical reflections on politics. He muses that he never allowed thought to interfere with his politics since "Politics and thought are radically different" (*L*, 119). He gets a bitter taste of unreliable supporters when, after feeding some seventy-five citizens doughnuts and cider at a rally, he discovers that at least forty have voted for his opponent. He moans, "Home endorsement, hard-boiled eggs and hot tears of reconciliation can never fool me again. They are as empty as the bass drum by which they are invariably accompanied" (*L*, 121–22).

Nye's ideas on change and growth in America are found mainly in "The Dubious Future" (*L*, 144–55) and "The Automatic Bell Boy" (*L*, 254–62). In the former, he is a bit skeptical of modern innovation, using the artificial methodology of fattening oysters for market as an example of man's tampering with natural processes. He concludes, "Our race is being tampered with not only by means of adulterous, political combinations and climatic changes, but even our methods of relaxation are productive of peculiar physical conditions, malformations and some more things of the same kind" (*L*, 147–48). In "The Automatic Bell Boy," however, his view of the future is somewhat more propitious. He mainly discusses the possibilities of advancements in electricity. Though admitting that Benjamin Franklin "might have considered it wisdom to go in when it rained" (*L*, 255) if he could have seen the present landscape strung with ugly electric wires, still Nye sees electricity as the answer to needs in life. Room service in hotels can be improved with electric message systems, and fire and police protection can be improved by means of electric alarm systems. With remarkable foresight, what Nye anticipates for hotel use is a computer that "remembers" messages and questions from guests and then provides answers at strategic times during the day. Nye's views of change and growth of technology in his day, then, are analogous to those of Mark Twain in *Life on the Mississippi* lauding progress in the South while nostalgically lamenting the loss of basic, natural interaction between man and his environment. Nye remains skeptical of progress, yet he is also ready to enjoy the fruits of modern inventions.

The essay entitled "The Sabbath Of A Great Author" (*L*, 64–68) presents some of Nye's strongest views on religion. Nye once said of his religious beliefs that he was "moderately liberal and free upon all religious matters" ("Polygamy as a Religious Duty," *R*, 419). He undoubtedly associated with the Indian's simple, "handmade" faith evident in "Squaw Jim's Religion" (*NB*, 247–48). That faith is "cheap and portable, and durable" (*NB*, 247). In his satires, Nye never attacks what he believed to be sound religion—only man's misconceptions of it and his erring practice of religion. As Levette J. Davidson has pointed out, "hypocrisy, affectation, and dishonesty are the targets for his satire."[97] We remember Nye's condemnation of Puritan religious oppressiveness and cruelty as shown in the *History of the United States*. Moreover, Nye had trouble reconciling the Old Testament God of wrath and jealousy with the Christian view of a God of love and mercy. In the *Ludlow* essay "The Sabbath Of A Great Author," he clearly states his position: "I like to go [to church] and hear about God's love, but I am rarely benefited by a discourse which enlarges upon his jealousy. When I am told also that God spares no pains in getting even with people, I not only do not enjoy the information, but I would sit up till a late hour at night to doubt it" (*L*, 66). Nye's religion, then, was a practical one that stressed the love, understanding, and forgiving nature of God. Doctrinal considerations were a waste of time for him. A doctrinaire sermon fatigued him "on account of the mental reservations [he] made along through it" (*L*, 66). Preachers who propounded their own dogmatic interpretations of scriptures disenchanted him. People who performed inhumane or irrational acts in the name of religion disgusted him.

As in all Nye's works, what occupies stage center in *Ludlow* is human nature. The book is a rich portraiture of people, from the North Carolina farmer who discusses his summer boarders (*L*, 123–33) to the bewildered visitor in Manhattan who cringes over the reckless teamsters on Broadway. In fact, the penultimate selection in *Ludlow* is a letter of advice to Nye's mythical son Henry in which Nye comments on human nature, especially as it is found at its worst in Gotham:

> This is a good town to study human nature in, Henry, and you would do well to come here before your vacation is over, just to see what kind of people the Lord allows to encumber the earth. It will show you how many human brutes there are loose in the world who don't try any longer to appear decent when they think their identity is swallowed up in the multitude of a great city. There are just as selfish folks in the smaller towns, but they are afraid to give themselves up to it, because somebody in the crowd would be sure to recognize them. Here a man has the advantage of a perpetual NOM DE PLUME, and he is tempted to see how pusillanimous he can be even when he is just here on a visit. (*L*, 252–53)

The touch of skepticism, always characteristic of Nye, carries through, then, to his last work. There is no discernible mellowing in this last book, though the essays he selected do present a balanced, variegated picture of life in its many phases. The various selections run in mood from pensive to frivolous.

Reprints of Nye's works and other posthumous collections are too numerous to discuss individually here, but the point must be made that Nye's publishers capitalized on his fame and turned out Nye books for some years after his death. A few of the late books produced are worth a brief discussion.

Not to be confused with *Nye and Riley's Railway Guide* or its reprint entitled *Fun, Wit, and Humor by Bill Nye and James Whitcomb Riley* was a book brought out by the W. B. Conkey Company of Chicago in 1901 entitled *Nye and Riley's Wit and Humor*. The volume begins with four poems by Riley before launching into a second section entitled "Bill Nye's Grim Jokes," which consists of over five hundred pages of Nye's essays, sketches, and anecdotes mainly culled from *Bill Nye and Boomerang, Forty Liars*, and *Bill Nye's Chestnuts*. The same pieces by Nye, minus Riley's poems, were also issued by the Conkey Company as *Bill Nye's Grim Jokes*.[98] A preface, "Piazza to the Third Volume," is identical to the one that appears in *Baled Hay*, Nye's third book. Since both *Wit and Humor* and *Grim Jokes* are essentially random reprints of pieces from Nye's earlier works, there is nothing particularly distinguished about them. They were merely publishing house enterprises to make money.

Though not posthumous, two books published by Ward, Lock, and Company of London probably in the middle to late 1880s[99] anticipate the 1903 publishing of *The Funny Fellow's Grab-Bag*, and thus merit some discussion. The two works are *Boomerang Shots* and *Hits and Skits*. Both are six-penny pamphlet miscellanies containing random selections from Nye's early books and a few selections apparently published for the first time in book form. The contents of *Boomerang Shots*, the first of the two books issued, are grouped under the headings "The Funny Editor," "The Wild Western Wit," "The Merry Miners," "The Very Last Mohicans," "Sweet Home and 'The Suite,'" "Trying A Jury," "Cow-Boy And Capers," and "Our Comic Columns," most of the headings and selections obviously reflecting Nye's Western period of 1876–1883. Much of this book is apparently taken from the daily or weekly *Boomerang* columns. Some of the material—primarily the one-liners, brief news items, and other space fillers—is undoubtedly not by Nye,[100] though likely selected or arranged by him for publication in the book.

The other London volume, *Hits and Skits*, is advertised on the title page as being by the "author of 'Boomerang Shots,'" and also carries an epigraph that explains the title: "You've but to choose your special bit;/The Hits are skittish, and each Skit's a hit." Though not so Western in setting and flavor as *Boomerang Shots*, most of the pieces are taken from *Bill Nye and Boomerang*, Nye's first book, or were newspaper columns that he later included in *Remarks*. Subject matter runs the gamut from "The Nocturnal Cow" to the satirical article "Health Food." Again, there are some filler squibs—though not as many as in *Boomerang Shots*—that were written by someone else and just collected and sometimes introduced by Nye.

The posthumous *Funny Fellow's Grab-Bag* (1903),[101] another paperback volume, is somewhat similar in form to these two precursors, though there is a more sizeable body of material (close to half the book) not written by Nye. In fact, the cover lists the work as being "By Bill Nye. And Other Funny Men," though these other writers remain anonymous. The book consists of seven signed articles by Nye, a number of unsigned articles by other contributors, and several pages of short anecdotes (also unsigned).

The Nye pieces in *Grab-Bag* are taken largely from Nye's latest period of writing, most being reprints of columns from the *New York World* and the American Press Humorists Association syndicate. In the various pieces, Nye discusses—with typical cutting wit—foreign emigrants, the smuggling of contraband into the United States, the workings of the New York Custom House, the deceptions of phrenology, ballet, a fortuitous case of smallpox in a mining camp, and the wretched verse of a newspaper poetaster. The whole book is a potpourri designed for newsstand or railroad depot distribution—an appealing book for travelers and people wanting leisurely parlor or bedside reading.

CHAPTER 7

A Word of Appraisal

NYE, according to Walter Blair, was "about the last man in the nineteenth-century humorous school to win popularity."[1] In his writings Nye differed from many of the earlier humorists in his school, Blair points out, by not "setting up a kind of character," by eschewing "the weird spelling and queer grammar," and by being far less political in his writings.[2] Furthermore, Blair states, Nye achieved a versatility which the earlier humorists such as Henry Wheeler Shaw, Charles Farrar Browne, and David Ross Locke lacked; Nye and the later humorists borrowed from humorists of all sections of the country, and thus there is in Nye a discernible culmination of many different traits once considered sectional.[3] Blair also senses a distinctive dual tone in Nye: he

one moment played the role of a fool, the next moment talked straight from the shoulder with only a hint of humorous intention here and there in his phrasing. . . . If a fool character authored one paragraph, a horse-sense character was as likely as not to author the next, and so on to the end of the piece. Sometimes in a single paragraph the two kinds of minds would show up in alternate sentences.[4]

Such is the appraisal of a noted modern specialist on Nye and American humor. With Blair's critique of Nye in mind, it is fruitful to turn to nineteenth-century criticism to ascertain what Nye's contemporaries thought of him, as well as to examine other twentieth-century reaction to a once major humorist who is now hardly ever read and whose name is unknown to so many.

I Critical Reception: The Nineteenth Century

Nye's contemporaries mostly praised both him and the state of American humor in the late nineteenth century. Mark Twain, though not without jealousy of Nye while Nye was alive,[5] could later safely

pronounce him a "real humorist, that gentle, good soul."[6] Julian Hawthorne, in 1891, called Nye "one of the most popular comic writers,"[7]
and, as previously quoted, Will M. Clemens said as early as 1882, when
Nye had just published his first book: "Bill Nye has, during the past
two years, written a larger quantity and a better quality of first-class,
genuine humor, than any other funny man in America."[8] The *Colorado Springs Gazette*, in an 1890 review of one of Nye's lectures, spoke
of him as "undoubtedly the most popular humorist and wit to-day
before the American public."[9] The *Denver Republican* offered this
appraisal in reviewing a Nye-Burbank performance in 1893:

> Nye is the most original humorist since the days of Artemus Ward. He has
> dealt in humor as a merchant deals in material commodities. The humorous
> fecundity of that bald head of his has been something remarkable. He has
> written constantly. He has done newspaper hack work in addition to his other
> literary labors; and though genius in the traces generally fails of success, his
> abundant humor has been perennially good.
> Probably in his writings Nye was funnier in the old days than he is now;
> he has begun to sacrifice fun, to some extent, to literary polish. But he is
> doubly a humorist—one in his writings and one upon the platform, and in
> the latter capacity he is at his best. His funny thoughts are then a hundred
> per cent funnier than they read, from the inimitable drollery of his delivery
> and the mock solemnity of his presence.[10]

Other critics singled out the nature and specific traits of Nye's
humor. An anonymous writer for *The Critic* felt that Nye's strength
"lies in the homeliness of his style. To my thinking some of the funniest
things he says are those which apparently cost him the least effort. It
is the simple statement of what he has to say, in the language and from
the point of view of the common people."[11] The *Colorado Springs
Gazette* claimed, "It is almost impossible to describe the quaint, original style of the humorist upon the stage. . . . Nye's dry wit . . . proved
most fascinating to the audience. . . ."[12] Publisher J. B. Lippincott
appraised Nye's writings as being "devoid of pathos and feeling" and
having "a certain hardness which is open to unfavorable literary criticism; and yet they show a remarkable insight into human nature, and
a keen perception of the humorous side of everyday life."[13] And lecture
partner James Whitcomb Riley addressed the "quaintness and whim-
sicality" of Nye's humor as being "the notable thing about him. It was
unaccountable upon any particular theory. It just seemed natural for
his mind to work at that gait."[14]

Nye's death in 1896 prompted a spate of praiseful testimonials and reevaluative criticism. The *New York World* spoke of Nye as "an exceedingly kind-hearted and generous man."[15] The *World* printed a tribute to Nye by Riley, who recalled of his former partner, "He was unselfish, wholly so, and I am heartened by recalling the always patient strength and gentleness of this true man, the unfailing hope and cheer and faith of his child-heart. . . ."[16] The *San Francisco Examiner* ran a lengthy front-page story on Nye's life and death and also a major editorial on "Edgar W. Nye, The Man Without An Enemy." The former article boasted, "His originality and felicity attracted general attention, and nearly every important newspaper in the land copies his sketches and comments."[17] The editorial, perhaps written by publisher William Randolph Hurst, stressed Nye's persistent humor, often written in adversity. Literarily, the editorial commented,

In his field of literary effort Nye stood not only without a peer, but without a rival. There is none now who can fill the vacancy. Others have tried, flashed across the sky—a rocket—and have been seen no more. Where these failed Nye kept on unflagging. The fountain of his wit never ran dry. Week after week, and year after year, his letters have appeared in the daily papers, always bubbling with fun, but yet with the grain of wisdom concealed under every jest and a keen perception of humanity apparent in every grotesque figure. Nye was artistic. He knew just how far to carry a conceit to make it most effective.[18]

The *New York Times* called Nye "one of the best-known American humorists," and concluded, "His quaint, good-natured, broadly-exaggerating writings gave him a large clientage among the newspaper readers and lecture attendants. While his humor was pronouncedly aggressive and distinctly American, his lectures and writings received a very warm reception in England and other foreign countries."[19]

Some of his contemporaries, of course, were not so laudatory of Nye. Poet E. A. Robinson's reaction can be cited as representative of criticism that frowned on Nye for not being more genteel and schooled. Robinson, who became upset when Nye was engaged to write for *The Century Illustrated Monthly Magazine*, charged, "It strikes me that they are making a mistake in admitting the latter [Nye], unless he changes his usual tone; but then, I may be prejudiced against him with no adequate reason. It always struck me, though, that he is a trifle coarse for such a periodical as the *Century* holds itself up to be."[20] Robinson went on to say that readers look for Nye and "rather enjoy" him in publications such as the "Sunday *Herald* or *Globe*," but "when he jumps into the higher regions of literature, one feels doubtful as to the results."[21]

Nevertheless, most of Nye's contemporary readers, lecture audiences, and the critics themselves, recognized and applauded his comic genius. Most of them agreed that his quaint methods and refreshing wit—especially the incongruous yoking of thought and diction—were among the best of the age.

II *Critical Reception: The Twentieth Century*

It became obvious early in the century that Nye's reputation was moribund. In 1906, just ten years after Nye's death, Mark Twain looked back on the late nineteenth-century humorists and found no survivors. He referred to an anthology of the humorists as a "cemetery": "Each and every one of [them] rose in my time, became conspicuous and popular, and by and by vanished."[22] Twain, though obviously biased, felt that Nye and others died because they were "mere humorists" instead of being preachers too. Twain believed the "preaching" had caused his own survival.[23] O. N. Gibson would agree with Twain's assessment, viewing Nye (though incorrectly) as too pure a humorist:

Pure humor is evanescent, ephemeral. As an alloy it gives luster and permanence to other literary forms but unmixed with more enduring material, it is apt to lose both its worth and charm.

This may in some measure, account for the rapidity with which Nye's fame is declining. He was a humorist, purely and simply. He possessed no poetic gift, no prophetic insight. He had no dogma to proclaim, no theory to expound. He understood his talents, and their limitations. He acknowledged no graver purpose, claimed no higher mission, than just to make men laugh; not bitterly, nor contemptuously, nor cynically, nor unkindly, but good humoredly, generously, with simple, genial and spontaneous mirth.[24]

William Dean Howells also spoke of the decline of Nye and other humorists of his school. Howells regretted their demise, calling them "true astral bodies" and wishing in vain that "their line may never end."[25] Thus, from the early part of the twentieth century critics have had to approach Nye as part of a vanishing tradition, viewing him as an important humorist and comic realist, but one whose reputation—unlike Mark Twain's—was rapidly declining.

In the early twentieth century there were still sentimental critics such as publisher William Webster Ellsworth who spoke of Nye as having been a "sweet-natured, kindly humorist, with a delightful twist to his fun."[26] But others addressed themselves to the nature of Nye's humor, his techniques, and the Nye legacy. In a major reappraisal of Nye's humor, Albert E. Hancock in 1903 stated that the essence of his comedy was his imaginative treatment of commonplace facts.[27] Though Hancock admits there is a certain amount of junk humor in Nye, he also discerns "a keen intellectual perception in Nye's humor at its best. . . ."[28] Viewing Nye as a "genius at antithesis," Hancock elaborates: "He perceived the detail which fits an artistic purpose—the unexpected detail which brings a trifle into bold relief, which subtly debases dignity, or which sheds the flash-light of truth on a humbug." Finally, Hancock speaks of the "current of pathos and sympathetic humanity" that he detects "flowing unostentatiously and noiselessly in the depths" of Nye's humor.

Edmund H. Eitel believed that the secret of Nye's humor lay in "surprises, in freaks of the imagination."[29] Turn of the century critic and literary historian James L. Ford, in appraising the whole field of nineteenth-century American humorists, saw Nye as succeeding Mark Twain as the leader of the school of platform funny men, when Twain turned his attention to other kinds of literary pursuit. Though Nye had a serious, philosophical vein, Ford concedes, "his strong point was his gift of comical expression, in which art he had few equals."[30] Ford calls Nye's "staying power" in his own time remarkable: "Only one who has gained his bread by humorous composition can really appreciate the talents which enabled this quaint writer to turn out at regular intervals a prodigious quantity of matter, whose average excellence was very high."[31] When Nye died, Ford opines, "there died also the school of which he was a leader. He was the last of his race, or, to speak more accurately, he was the last to maintain the supremacy of his school against all others."[32]

W. E. Chaplin, who had served with Nye on the *Laramie Sentinel* and *Boomerang*, analyzed the humor of his erstwhile famous associate, calling it "keen, spontaneous, satirical," and recognizing the vitriolic sarcasm in Nye's satiric jabs when he was attacked.[33] He felt that Nye's strongest suit lay in his dual tone—the "quick change from the sublime to the ridiculous."[34] Chaplin recalled some thirty years after Nye's death that

In his city work [for the *Laramie Sentinel*] Nye's humor began to unfold. In all that he wrote there was a vein running from the sublime to the ridiculous and his rapid change from one to the other was the underlying power that made his sketches popular with the American people. The most common-place item was given a turn that made the reader smile and there was laughter all through the local columns of the *Sentinel*, a paper that had been as wise as an owl and as sober as a judge.[35]

Two other former friends and associates of Nye, Eugene Debs and William Lightfoot Visscher, added their opinions on the key to Nye's comic writing. Debs considered Nye a philosopher: "Beneath his flow of humor there was a sub-stratum of serious meditation. He was the master of pathos as well as the lord of laughter."[36] Debs also recalled Nye's talent of finding humor in almost every situation: "To the keen and searching eye of Bill Nye there was a humorous side to everything. Humor was to him the essence of wisdom, the savor of life. He delighted in expressing himself and interpreting his friends in terms of kindly, genial, good-natured humor. If he was vexed for a moment, he found relief in seeking out the funny side of his vexation so that he might laugh it away."[37] Visscher especially remembered Nye's idiosyncratic personal demeanor, which prompted humorous reactions from his audiences: "One of Nye's funniest peculiarities was his solemnity of look and sepulchral voice when he was saying something that he knew to be unusually humorous. At such times he had a queer sort of cross-eyed glint leftward."[38] Visscher goes on to point out that Nye's humorous method frequently duped people because they did not realize he was being facetious. "Thus his humor was not always fully appreciated by audiences when he 'lectured.'"[39]

Canadian critic Stephen Leacock singled out Nye's "deliberate assumption of simplicity,"[40] his "assumption of an inspired and enthusiastic idiocy,"[41] as chief traits of his humorous pose, the latter trait also being stressed by George F. Whicher.[42] Leacock placed Nye with that "brilliant and distinctive group of the middle and later nineteenth century . . . who first made American humor a distinct and truly national branch of literature."[43] Commenting on the flaws and strengths of Nye's humor, Leacock continues, "His work, like that of all the school, is often disfigured by the haste of its casual production and by its frequent reliance upon the cheap devices of verbal form. But the real merit of it lies in its essential point of view—broad, kindly, and human, and reflecting the new American analysis of traditional and conventional ideas."[44]

Toward the middle of the twentieth century, Douglas C. McMurtrie compared Nye's newspaper humor with that of Will Rogers, stressing that Nye's humor was "entirely dependent on his own personality" and pointing out that "Nye's specialty was enlarging on some local item of trivial importance."[45]

Since mid-century there has not been a great deal of critical attention to Nye alone, though his whole school of humor has undergone reevaluation. Notable exceptions are Louis Hasley's *The Best of Bill Nye's Humor* (1968), an edition of selections from Nye with appreciative critical introduction; the present author's *Bill Nye: The Western Writings*, a monograph examining the Western phase and flavor of Nye's works, including the influence of the West on his humor; and the scholarship of T. A. Larson. In an excellent article "Laramie's Bill Nye," Larson reviews the history of Nye's career in Laramie and comments on his humor in general. In his ponderous *History of Wyoming*, Larson devotes a number of pages throughout the book to Nye's literary, social, and political role in the developing Territory of Wyoming in the 1870s and 1880s. Most significant among Larson's works on Nye, however, is his anthology with historical-critical introduction, *Bill Nye's Western Humor*.[46] He precedes his selections from Nye's works with the just claim that though tastes have changed since Nye's day, "much that he wrote still transmits to the contemporary reader the whimsy and the idiocy that make people laugh. In addition, it is of value to the social historian since it pictures frontier customs and characters and illuminates the popular taste of the 1880s and 1890s."[47]

Aside from Hasley, Kesterson, and Larson, criticism on Nye since 1950 has found its way into an occasional masters thesis,[48] newspaper feature,[49] and book on American literature or American humor. Among the last, Van Wyck Brooks has alluded to Nye's being a newspaper humorist "full of New England rural feeling," despite his Western upbringing.[50] Jesse Bier, in *The Rise and Fall of American Humor*, discusses Nye's techniques and caustic tone as being representative of his school of realistic critics, and points to Nye's influence on Finley Peter Dunne, the popular turn-of-the-century humorist and creator of Mr. Dooley.[51] C. Carroll Hollis, in "Rural Humor of the Late Nineteenth Century," refers to Nye's transcending the newspaper role because of his widespread fame, and recalls that Nye's book sales "were well over five million."[52] Jay Martin, in an essay on the humor of Ambrose Bierce, somewhat mistakenly classes Nye with Josh Billings and John Phoenix as practitioners of the epigram.[53] Surprisingly and disappointingly—considering Walter Blair's prominent work on Nye earlier in the twentieth century—his and Hamlin Hill's recent *America's Humor from Poor Richard to Doonesbury* relegates Nye and forty other "Phunny Phellows" to a footnote, while Charles Farrar Browne, Henry Wheeler Shaw, David Ross Locke, and Charles H. Smith are discussed in some detail.[54]

III   *Is Bill Nye Still Funny?*

Of course, Nye can always be read with historical interest. His humorous sketches, essays, and miscellaneous writings inform the modern reader about late nineteenth-century American culture. But a central question lingers: Is he still funny today? Can Nye be read as a humorist with appeal to a modern audience?

"Humor changes styles," reminds G. D. Eaton in a review of Nye's appeal,[55] and thus much that was funny to Nye's contemporaries is no more. T. A. Larson agrees: "Early in the 20th century Nye's humor became 'dated,' and much that must have been funny when written lost its punch. Perhaps one-half of what Nye wrote was funny when published. Now only one-tenth has much appeal."[56]

A full appreciation of Nye's humor by the modern reader is discouraged by the form of most of his works—short sketches and vignettes designed for newspaper publication or platform utterances. How "readable," we might ask, will a collection of the newspaper articles of Art Buchwald or Irma Bombeck be a century from now? Carroll Hollis agrees that a major problem in appreciating Nye occurs when the modern reader is faced with an entire book of his short, unrelated pieces:

with all the humor, skill, and critical perception at Nye's command, and with the most sympathetic and expectant audience any humorist could ask for, still it is almost impossible to read one of his books all the way through. One could read the first and the second with responsive chuckles, but the third would seem less funny, for the fourth one would have to concentrate to keep the mind from wandering, for the fifth one might falter but proceed, with occasional skimming, by the sixth one would know what was going to happen as soon as one determined the subject matter, by the seventh, if one got that far, the formula would be so patently obvious that one would put the book aside with a sigh of disappointment.[57]

Had Nye ventured into the realm of the satiric novel or the short story, or done more with playwriting, undoubtedly he would be more appealing to modern readers than he is.

Despite the drawbacks, there is still enjoyment in him. Certainly more than local chauvinism has prompted the *Laramie Boomerang* to reprint Nye's columns over the last few years. Moreover, there is in Nye's writings—despite some purely topical essays—a universality of subject and modernity of tone, as Jesse Bier has pointed out in his reassessment of the funny men in general.[58] Nye's ability to see irony in almost everything and his sardonic tone of voice are certainly in vogue in the late twentieth century. And he eschews many of the antiquated stock subjects and devices of the literary comedians. As the anonymous appraiser in the *New Encyclopaedia Britannica* points out, Nye "has worn better than some of his humorous contemporaries" because he avoids the abundant political satire and the conscious devices of misspelling, faulty grammar, and distorted diction of many of his school. Furthermore, writing as his own self, rather than assuming the role of a folksy persona, "Nye reveals his own kindly but droll nature."[59]

Nye at his best is indeed still funny. The sidesplitting inanities of a "Twombley's Tale," the absurd biographies of historical personages, the wittily perceptive analyses of human nature, and the droll comments on everything from Broadway to boxing are all enduring. Perhaps T. A. Larson has stated it best: "much that he wrote still transmits to the contemporary reader the whimsy and the idiocy that make people laugh."[60]

Notes and References

Many of the primary works cited throughout this book are newspaper columns written for the *New York World* or syndicated by the American Press Humorists Association. References to those articles appear in the notes, rather than the text, because of the amount of textual space that would be required for the title of the article, name of newspaper, date, etc. Furthermore, I have used almost entirely the *New York World* and the *San Francisco Examiner* as my source newspapers for the period of Nye's journalism (1886–1896); Nye wrote fairly exclusively for the *World* from 1886 to 1891, and the *Examiner* is one of the most currently accessible newspapers containing Nye's writings after he severed his weekly contact with the *World* in June 1891 and syndicated his column. I have abbreviated the titles of these two newspapers throughout as *World* and *Examiner*.

Transcripts of a large collection of Nye's letters are located in the Bill Nye Collection, Hebard Room of the Coe Library at the University of Wyoming. References to letters in this collection are labeled "Hebard letters." Other items in the collection, such as newspaper articles about Nye, are cited as being in the "Hebard file."

Preface

1. Dan Chiszar, "U.S. Has Forgotten Bill Nye, Once Among Noted Humorists," *Dallas Times Herald*, 7 December 1978, sec. A, p. 39.

2. Will M. Clemens, "Bill Nye," in *Famous Funny Fellows* (Cleveland: William W. Williams, 1882), p. 117.

3. Robert Ford, "Bill Nye," in *American Humourists* (London: Alexander Gardner, 1897), p. 226.

4. [Walter McDougall], "Bill Nye As Seen By Walt McDougall," in "Bill Nye—The Inimitable: His Work And His Personality," *Book Lovers Magazine*, 1 (June 1903), 604.

Chapter One

1. "Nye As A Millionnaire," *Examiner*, 16 September 1894, p. 22.

2. For a brief, but informative account of Nye's mother, see Fred C. Kelly, "Bill Nye's Mother," *Colliers*, 10 April 1915, p. 22.

3. The best biographical sources on Nye's early years, sources to which I am indebted throughout this chapter, are Stephen Leacock, "Nye, Edgar

Wilson," *Dictionary of American Biography,* ed. Dumas Malone (New York: Scribner's, 1934), XIII, 598–600; Frank Wilson Nye, ed., *Bill Nye: His Own Life Story* (New York: Century, 1926); and John Francis Sprague, "Edgar Wilson Nye," *Collections of the Piscataquis County Historical Society* (Dover, Maine: Observer Press, 1910), I, 147–53. I am especially indebted throughout this study to Frank Nye's *Bill Nye: His Own Life Story,* the nearest approach to an autobiography-biography of Nye in print. This book is hereafter cited as F. W. Nye.

4. "Where He First Met His Parents," in *Nye and Riley's Railway Guide* (Chicago: Dearborn Publishing, 1888), p. 3; hereafter cited in the text as *RG.*

5. F. W. Nye, p. 16.

6. "Back Where Nye Was Riz," *Examiner,* 2 December 1894, p. 18.

7. "In A Superior Country," *Examiner,* 13 March 1892, p. 17.

8. Ibid.

9. Ibid.

10. For the full account of how Nye assumed his pseudonym, see his letter to Melville D. Landon (Eli Perkins) in *Kings of the Platform and Pulpit* (Chicago: Werner, 1895), pp. 308–9.

11. F. W. Nye, p. 94.

12. The best treatment of Fanny Nye is found in Augusta Prescott, "The Family of a Humorist," *The Ladies' Home Journal,* March 1895, p. 5.

13. *Remarks* (Chicago: Davis, 1887), pp. 180, 182; hereafter cited in the text as *R.*

14. F. W. Nye, p. 117.

15. Walter Blair, "The Popularity of Nineteenth-Century American Humorists," *American Literature,* 3 (May 1931), 192.

16. Walter Blair, "The Background of Bill Nye in American Humor" (Ph. D. diss., University of Chicago, 1931), p. 124.

17. "Some Idle Thoughts," *Examiner,* 6 March 1892, p. 25.

18. *The Complete Works of James Whitcomb Riley* (New York: Harper and Brothers, 1916), VI, 1704.

19. W. E. Chaplin, "Bill Nye," *The Frontier,* 11 (March 1931), 223.

20. "Edgar W. Nye: The Man Without An Enemy," *Examiner,* 23 February 1896, p. 6.

Chapter Two

1. "Bankrupt Sale Of A Circus," in *Bill Nye and Boomerang; or The Tale of a Meek-Eyed Mule, and Other Literary Gems* (Chicago: Belford, Clarke, 1881), p. 216; hereafter cited in the text as *NB,* usually preceded by the title of the specific short piece in question.

2. For a concentrated study of the Western phase of Nye's career see my *Bill Nye: The Western Writings* (Boise: Boise State University, 1976).

3. For the most thorough treatments of Nye's journalistic career in Laramie see W. E. Chaplin's articles: "Bill Nye in Laramie," in *Second Biennial Report, State Historian of Wyoming* (Sheridan: Mills, 1921–1923), pp. 142–58; "Some of the Early Newspapers of Wyoming," in *Wyoming Historical Society Miscellanies* (Laramie: Laramie Republican, 1919), pp. 7–24; "Some Wyoming Editors I Have Known," *Annals of Wyoming* 18 (January 1946), 79–87. See also T. A. Larson, "Laramie's Bill Nye," in *The Denver West— 1952 Brand Book* (Denver: The Westerners, 1953), pp. 34–56.

4. Chaplin, "Bill Nye In Laramie," p. 144.

5. Ibid., pp. 142–43.

6. Levette J. Davidson, "'Bill' Nye And The Denver Tribune," *The Colorado Magazine*, 4 (January 1927), 13–18.

7. Ibid., pp. 13–14.

8. Ibid., p. 17.

9. Chaplin, "Bill Nye In Laramie," p. 144.

10. Quoted from *Cheyenne Daily Sun* for 16 March 1881 (Hebard file, p. 14) since *Boomerang* files from Nye's time are not extant.

11. Clemens, *Famous Funny Fellows*, p. 117.

12. See Chaplin, "Some Wyoming Editors I Have Known," p. 82, and Frank Luther Mott, *American Journalism, A History: 1690-1960* (New York: Macmillan, 1962), p. 483.

13. See Larson, "Laramie's Bill Nye," p. 45, for details of Nye's business closure with the *Boomerang* corporation.

14. "The Editorial Lamp," in *Baled Hay: A Drier Book Than Walt Whitman's "Leaves o' Grass"* (Chicago: Belford, Clarke, 1884), pp. 169–70; hereafter cited in the text as *BH*, usually preceded by the title of the specific short piece in question.

15. "Good Advice Given Away," *Examiner*, 14 August 1892, p. 17.

16. "The Man Who Licks the Editor," in *Forty Liars, And Other Lies* (Chicago: Belford, Clarke, 1882), pp. 199–200; hereafter cited in the text as *FL*, usually preceded by the title of the specific short piece in question.

17. Larson, "Laramie's Bill Nye," p. 41.

18. Ibid., p. 42.

19. "English As She Is Wrote," *Examiner*, 12 August 1894, p. 14.

20. Ibid.

21. See also "The Reporters Were There," *World*, 15 September 1889, p. 23.

22. Clemens, *Famous Funny Fellows*, p. 119.

23. The essay appears in three versions: "Suggestions For A School Of Journalism," *NB*, pp. 31–35, "The Newspaper," *R*, pp. 421–27, and "Bill Nye Has A Young Idea," *World*, 3 June 1888, p. 13.

24. See "The Newspaper" and "Bill Nye Has A Young Idea."

25. Also see "Bill Nye Has A Young Idea."

26. Ibid.

27. Larson, "Laramie's Bill Nye," p. 46.

28. Ibid.

29. Ibid.

30. Diane E. Heestand, "The Writing of Bill Nye in Laramie" (M.A. thesis, University of Wyoming, 1968), p. 17.

31. Ethel L. Lindsey, "Edgar Wilson Nye And American Humor" (M.A. thesis, University of Wyoming, 1929), pp. 47–48.

32. Also see "Gingerbread Poems And Cold Pickled Facts," NB, pp. 152–55.

33. See such articles as "A Ute Presidential Convention," NB, pp. 183–89; "Sitting Bull. His Speech Before the Sioux Common Council," FL, pp. 15–18; "Oration. Delivered July 4th, By Pop-Eyed Caterpillar, of the Ute Nation," FL, pp. 70–75; "The Fourth Among the Utes," FL, pp. 168–69; "Circular From Colorow," FL, pp. 190–92; "New Years Among the Utes," FL, pp. 242–45; "Sic Semper Gloria Colorow," FL, pp. 273–74; and other pieces scattered throughout Nye's books and newspaper columns.

34. See "The Indian Orator," R, pp. 443–44; "Chipeta's Address to the Utes," BH, pp. 37–39; and Colorow's speeches appearing throughout Nye's early works.

35. "Lo, With Pen In Hand," Examiner, 11 September 1892, p. 17.

36. T. A. Larson, History of Wyoming (Lincoln: University of Nebraska Press, 1965), p. 224.

37. Ibid., p. 110.

38. Ibid., p. 141.

39. As late as 1890, in fact, Nye devoted an entire column in the Sunday World to reviewing a biography of the Younger brothers ("Nye Reviews A Book," 31 August 1890, p. 20).

40. For other essays on the bad man and violence of the West see "Correspondence. Dalles of the St. Croix, Sept. 8, 1880," NB, pp. 131–37; "A Frontier Incident," FL, pp. 117–20; "The Death of Big-Nose George," FL, pp. 194–95; and "The 'Hold-Up' Business," FL, pp. 210–12.

41. "How A Mine Is Worked," and "How They Salt A Claim," FL, pp. 58–60, 112–13; "Mining As A Science," BH, pp. 295–97; "The Miner At Home," and "My Mine," R, pp. 151–53, 183–84.

42. See the similar "Wants To Come," FL, pp. 277–78.

43. Larson, History of Wyoming, pp. 78–94.

44. "Bill Nye On Women's Rights," World, 10 November 1889, p. 28; "A Plea for the Votresses," Examiner, 19 August 1894, p. 15; "Bill Nye And the New Woman," Examiner, 5 May 1895, p. 22; and "William's Weird Wisdom," Examiner, 19 May 1895, p. 15 (in which he describes his introduction to Susan B. Anthony).

45. "Among the Unmatched," Examiner, 27 March 1892, p. 15.

46. "Nye Writes To His Son," Examiner, 6 August 1893, p. 12.

47. "Thoughts On Marriage," Examiner, 4 March 1894, p. 15.

48. Prescott, p. 5.
49. "Bloomers Are Good Things," *Examiner*, 13 October 1895, p. 21.
50. Larson, "Laramie's Bill Nye," p. 45.
51. For Nye's discussions of his disease, spiced with barbed comments about the doctors treating it, see "Spinal Meningitis" and "My Physician," *R*, pp. 122–24, 354–55.

Chapter Three

1. Blair, "The Background of Bill Nye," p. 21.
2. Ibid., p. 5.
3. Edmund H. Eitel, "Letters of Riley and Bill Nye," *Harper's Magazine*, 138 (March 1919), 474.
4. Stephen Leacock, "American Humor," *The Nineteenth Century*, 76 (August 1914), 446.
5. Chaplin, "Bill Nye In Laramie," p. 142.
6. Albert E. Hancock, "Bill Nye and His Work," *Book Lovers Magazine*, 1 (June 1903), 603.
7. Louis Hasley, "Introduction," in *The Best of Bill Nye's Humor* (New Haven: College and University Press, 1972), p. 23.
8. For discussions of the "Dear Henry" letters, see Blair, "The Background of Bill Nye," p. 26, and F. W. Nye, pp. 128–29.
9. For example, see "Onion Peelins," *NB*, pp. 285–86.
10. Davidson, p. 17.
11. Blair, "The Background of Bill Nye," p. 77.
12. "Nye's Deal In Stocks," *Examiner*, 24 September 1893, p. 13.
13. Davidson, p. 17.
14. The remark is attributed to John Dewey by F. W. Nye, p. xiii.
15. Chaplin, "Bill Nye," p. 224.
16. "Bill Nye And The Parson," *World*, 16 September 1888, p. 9.
17. "Nye Criticises A Critic," *Examiner*, 9 August 1891, p. 13.
18. For other unflattering comments on Wilde by Nye see "The Rag Carpet," "Rough On Oscar," "Chicago Custom House," "Let Bald-Headed Men Rejoice," *BH*, pp. 27, 177, 246, 289; "Bill Nye And Mr. Wilde," *Examiner*, 28 April 1895, p. 22.
19. Larson, "Laramie's Bill Nye," p. 43.
20. Blair, "The Background of Bill Nye," p. 51.
21. Ibid., p. 68.
22. Ibid., p. 31.
23. Eitel, p. 474.
24. "He Answers Questions," *Examiner*, 4 June 1893, p. 14.
25. "Nye At the Eden Musee," *World*, 2 November 1890, p. 23.
26. "The Joke Pure And Simple," *Examiner*, 7 October 1894, p. 26.

27. "Bill Nye Visits Canada," *Examiner*, 21 February 1892, p. 14.

28. "Bill Nye About Liars," *Examiner*, 21 June 1891, p. 13.

29. "It's A National Calamity," *Examiner*, 28 October 1894, p. 18.

30. Eugene V. Debs, *Riley, Nye & Field* (n.p., n.d.), p. 11.

31. Hancock, p. 603.

Chapter Four

1. F. W. Nye, p. 16.

2. Published separately as *A Howl In Rome* (Milwaukee?, ca. 1880).

3. "Day Of The Spell-binder Is Past, Says Nye," *Examiner*, 9 February 1896, p. 31.

4. Ibid.

5. See "Bill Nye In High Clover," *World*, 29 January 1888, p. 11; "Bill Nye On Banquets," *World*, 14 September 1890, p. 22; and "Bill Nye's Commencement," *Examiner*, 30 June 1895, p. 15.

6. Landon, pp. 312–14.

7. "From Rum to Socrates," *Examiner*, 13 August 1893, p. 12.

8. "Drawbacks Of Public Life," *NB*, pp. 64–65. For parodies of Indian Fourth of July speeches see "Oration Delivered July 4th By Pop-Eyed Caterpillar Of The Ute Nation" (*FL*, pp. 70–73), and "How The Glorious Fourth Was Celebrated At Whalen's Grove Last Year" (*Bill Nye's Chestnuts Old and New: Latest Gathering* [Chicago: Belford, Clarke, 1888], pp. 21–29); hereafter cited in the text as *C*. As Blair points out, Nye's burlesques of the Indian Fourth of July address "allowed him to attack not only contemporary eloquence, but also the current romantic conception of the Indian" ("The Background of Bill Nye," p. 58).

9. Blair, "Background of Bill Nye," p. 54.

10. Ibid., p. 56.

11. Ibid., p. 60.

12. "From The Greenroom," *Examiner*, 5 February 1893, p. 14.

13. Ibid.

14. For details of the Lyceum and early lecturing see Carl Bode, *The American Lyceum* (New York: Oxford University Press, 1956) and Cecil B. Hayes, *The American Lyceum: Its History And Contribution To Education* (Washington, D.C.: U.S. Government Printing Office, 1932).

15. Besides the two sources listed in the previous note, see Paul Fatout, *Mark Twain on the Lecture Circuit* (Bloomington: Indiana University Press, 1960); Pond's days with Redpath are treated on p. 193.

16. James B. Pond, *Eccentricities of Genius* (New York: G. W. Dillingham, 1900), p. 237.

17. Edgar W. Nye, letter to J. B. Pond, 9 March 1885 (Hebard letters).

18. "To Friend Way," 17 March 1885, in *Letters of Edgar Wilson Nye*

Now in the University of Wyoming Library, ed. Nixon Orwin Rush (Laramie: University of Wyoming Library, 1950), p. 9; this collection is hereafter cited as Rush.

19. Pond, p. 239.
20. Ibid., p. 240.
21. Edgar W. Nye, letter to J. B. Pond, 5 April 1886 (Hebard letters).
22. Debs, p. 2.
23. Marcus Dickey, *The Maturity of James Whitcomb Riley* (Indianapolis: Bobbs-Merrill, 1922), p. 216.
24. Ibid., pp. 234–35.
25. Eitel, p. 476.
26. See Dickey, pp. 215–19, for the fullest account of this occasion; also William Lyon Phelps, ed. *Letters of James Whitcomb Riley* (Indianapolis: Bobbs-Merrill, 1930), passim, and Peter Revell, *James Whitcomb Riley* (New York: Twayne, 1970), p. 22.
27. Dickey, pp. 239–42.
28. "Nye And Riley In Chicago," *Chicago Herald,* 16 February 1888 (article provided by UCLA Library).
29. Pond actually retained the major voice in the corporation. See his assessment of the agreement in *Eccentricities,* p. 241. Countless contract troubles developed with Walker and Riley (see Nye's letters, passim, in the Hebard letters).
30. Pond, pp. 241–42.
31. Ibid., p. 246.
32. Ibid., p. 247.
33. Eitel, p. 482.
34. Albert Bigelow Paine, *Mark Twain: A Biography* (New York: Harper and Brothers, 1912), III, 877; Revell, p. 40.
35. Pond, p. 249.
36. Ibid., p. 250.
37. Landon, p. 314.
38. Ibid.
39. Eitel, p. 482.
40. Revell, p. 114.
41. Dickey, p. 248.
42. Debs, pp. 9–10.
43. Phelps, p. 91.
44. Dickey, pp. 243–44.
45. Eitel, p. 479.
46. "Nye & Riley's Route. Season 1888–9" (lecture calendar, in Indiana University Library).
47. Eitel, p. 479.
48. F. W. Nye, pp. 234–35.
49. Debs, p. 10.

50. Edgar W. Nye, letter to J. B. Pond, 13 September 1895 (Hebard letters).

51. The Nye-Riley program card for their first performance under Pond's management appears in Landon, *Eccentricities*, p. 242.

52. Landon, pp. 314–25.

53. Souvenir program in the University of Virginia Library. Headlining Nye as "The Greatest Living Humorist," the program prints the bogus autobiographies that Nye and Riley wrote of each other, reprints press notices of Nye and Riley's past successes, and carries numerous advertisements and railroad schedules.

54. Pond, p. 242. The phrase was printed at the bottom of the program for 1889.

55. See Dickey for details, pp. 254–56.

56. Ibid., p. 258.

57. James Whitcomb Riley, "To Mrs. R. E. Jones," 27 February 1890, ed. Phelps, pp. 96–97.

58. Nye felt Riley was overly petty and self-seeking in their business relationship, especially concerning the percentage of profits Riley was to receive. He also resented Riley's longing for equal, if not top, billing, feeling that Riley should recognize Nye as the superior attraction on the circuit. Riley's inability to keep schedules straight and thus his constant need of Nye as "guide" also took its toll on Nye's patience. See Hebard letters, passim.

59. Edgar W. Nye, letter to J. B. Pond, 6 June 1891 (Hebard letters).

60. For details of the Nye-Burbank association, see F. W. Nye, passim.

61. "Wandering Willie," *Examiner*, 22 November 1891, p. 14; also see announcement in *Examiner* for 12 February 1893, p. 19, directly under Nye's column: "Bill Nye and A. P. Burbank, the celebrated entertainers. Metropolitan Temple, February 21st and 22d."

62. F. W. Nye, p. 297.

63. "Programme of the Bill Nye and Burbank Entertainment" (in the New York Public Library–Lincoln Center Library of Performing Arts).

64. See, for example, "Nye And Burbank," *Denver Republican*, 10 February 1893 (Hebard file).

65. Edgar W. Nye, letter to J. B. Pond, 6 June 1891 (Hebard letters).

66. Pond, p. 258.

67. "Freaks Of A Radiator," *Examiner*, 21 May 1893, p. 15.

68. F. W. Nye, p. 350.

69. "He Becomes An Outlaw," *Examiner*, 18 December 1892, p. 18.

70. "Bill Nye's Entertainment," *Colorado Springs Gazette*, 5 March 1890 (Hebard file).

71. "Bill Nye As A Lecturer," *World*, 2 December 1888, p. 17.

72. Ibid.

73. Reprinted among press quotes in the Nye-Riley souvenir program of 27 January 1890 (in the University of Virginia Library).

74. Ibid.

75. Mabell Shippie Clarke, "Edgar Wilson Nye," *The Writer*, 9 (March 1896), 34.

76. J. B. Lippincott, "Bill Nye As Viewed By His Publisher," in "Bill Nye—The Inimitable: His Work And His Personality," *Book Lovers Magazine*, 1 (June 1903), 605.

77. Dickey, pp. 236–37.

78. "Nye And Riley In Chicago."

79. Dickey, p. 253.

80. Ibid.

81. Eitel, p. 474.

82. "Bill Nye's Entertainment."

83. Eitel, p. 479.

84. When Nye began lecturing with Riley he was making about $300 a week on the platform ("Bill Nye And Whitcomb Riley," *World*, 25 November 1888, p. 16). His fortunes rose rapidly, however, and by the end of his second year of lectures with Riley, he was occasionally drawing as much as $1000 weekly (Dickey, p. 254). E. G. Edwards wrote in 1892 that Nye was earning as much as $25,000 to $30,000 a year from the platform "so that in the past four or five years Mr. Nye's income has equaled that of the greatest lawyers, and has been as large as the individual profits which many bankers and merchants have received from their businesses . . ." ("Nye, The Humanist" [nationally syndicated newspaper column], 17 January 1892).

85. All these tricks are recalled by Edmund Eitel, pp. 479–80.

86. "Lecturing On Indians," *Examiner*, 18 June 1893, p. 15.

87. Dickey, p. 253.

88. Ibid., p. 252.

89. "He Took Half An Acre," *Examiner*, 9 April 1893, p. 14.

90. "Lecturing On Indians," p. 15.

91. Edgar W. Nye, letter to [J. B. Pond?], 25 February 1888 (Hebard letters).

92. Edgar W. Nye, letter to J. B. Pond, 2 April 1890 (Hebard letters).

93. Pond, p. 254.

94. Eitel, p. 479.

95. Eitel, p. 473; Dickey, p. 245.

96. "Stories By A Lawyer," *Examiner*, 12 March 1893, p. 18.

97. See Debs, pp. 8–9. In a letter to J. B. Pond Nye writes pleadingly, "We have missed Mr. Riley somehow, and thereby lost our train. What is the matter? We do not even know where he is and if he is not sure of being at Schenectady tonight there is no use of my going" (Hebard letter, 25 December 18—?).

98. See Hebard letters, passim. Nye had to bargain with Pond constantly, threatening to resign from the tour if Pond did not pay him more or stop scheduling distant "one-nighters," or agree to promote Nye as the chief attraction of their tour.

99. Dickey, p. 252.

100. Dickey, p. 238; Phelps, p. 73.

101. "Bill Nye At The Capitol," *Examiner*, 10 January 1892, p. 16; Phelps, pp. 155–56 (letter of 18 January 1892).

102. Pond, p. 258.

103. "Lecturing On Indians," p. 15.

104. "Learning To Lecture," *Examiner*, 22 January 1893, p. 19. This is one of Nye's best essays on the art.

105. Examples of the latter are "A Thrilling Experience," pp. 131–33; "My Lecture Abroad," pp. 149–50 (Nye is just fantasizing; he has not lectured abroad at this point); and "A Collection Of Keys," pp. 383–84.

106. Eitel, p. 475.

107. Phelps, p. 60.

108. "New Books And New Editions," *Book Buyer*, February 1889, pp. 28-29.

109. Phelps, p. 86 (letter of 3 October 1888).

110. Blair, "The Background of Bill Nye," pp. 130–31.

111. Phelps, p. 187 (letter of 14 June 1883).

112. Eitel, p. 484.

Chapter Five

1. "Bill Nye's Weather Report," *World*, 12 December 1886, p. 17.

2. Ibid.

3. Edwards, p. 8.

4. See both F. W. Nye, passim, and Edwards, p. [8].

5. For an account of the Nye family in their Tompkinsville home, see "Bill Nye At His Home," *World*, 8 February 1891, p. 11.

6. F. W. Nye, p. 179.

7. [Walter McDougall], "Bill Nye As Seen By Walt McDougall," p. 604.

8. Ibid.

9. Ibid. reprinted in F. W. Nye, pp. 179–82.

10. F. W. Nye, pp. 182–83.

11. "Bill Nye Visits Paris," *World*, 7 July 1889, p. 9.

12. "Bill Nye's Parisian Notes," *World*, 28 July 1889, p. 15.

13. "Bill Nye Enjoying Paris," *World*, 14 July 1889, p. 15.

14. "Bill Nye At A Paris Musee," *World*, 21 July 1889, p. 15.

15. "Bill Nye Arrested In Paris," *World*, 11 August 1889, p. 17.

16. "Bill Nye And Royalty," *World*, 18 August 1889, p. 9.

17. "Bill Nye And M'Allister," *World*, 12 May 1889, p. 21; "Left Out Of The '150'," *Examiner*, 20 March, 1892, p. 17; "The Harlem Chamois," *World*, 25 January 1891, p. 25.

18. "Left Out Of The '150'."

19. "Bill Nye And M'Allister."

20. "Bill Nye Speaks Out," *World*, 29 June 1890, p. 23.

21. "On Living In New York," *World*, 19 October 1890, p. 27.

22. "Render Fealty To Nye," *Examiner*, 6 November 1892, p. 15.

23. "Bill Nye Takes A Day Off," *World*, 13 July 1890, p. 22.

24. "Our Baseball Literature," *World*, 29 April 1888, p. 21; "Bill Nye At Jerome Park," *World*, 23 June 1889, p. 25.

25. "Sullivan As Litterateur," *World*, 25 November 1888, p. 13.

26. "William Nye Invests In A Brand-New Comet," *Examiner*, 12 January 1896, p. 22; "Bill Nye Meets A Chemist," *World*, 16 January 1887, p. 10; "Bill Nye On Electricity," *World*, 6 May 1888, p. 9; "Bill Nye As A Scientist," *World*, 20 November 1887, p. 9.

27. "Bill Nye As An Art Critic," *World*, 19 June 1887, p. 9.

28. "Bill Nye's Idea Of Art," *World*, 15 December 1889, p. 21.

29. "Baled Hay In Old England," *Examiner*, 29 October 1893, pp. 11–12.

30. Ibid., p. 12.

31. "Typical Tale Of The South," *Examiner*, 18 November 1894, p. 26.

32. "Nye Treats Of Widowers," *Examiner*, 2 June 1895, p. 15.

33. "Mr. William Nye Poses As Poet And Pedant," *Examiner*, 2 February 1896, p. 18.

34. "On The Pneumatic Tire," *Examiner*, 27 August 1893, p. 13.

35. "Mr. William Nye Poses As Poet And Pedant."

36. Also see "A New Poet" (*BH*, pp. 78–80).

37. "In Iowa And Illinois," *Examiner*, 15 January 1893, p. 14.

38. "Mr. William Nye Poses As Poet And Pedant."

39. "Faith In Witch Hazel," *Examiner*, 31 July 1892, p. 14.

40. "Bill Nye On Copyright," *World*, 27 November 1887, p. 9.

41. "Ten Per Cent Royalty," *Examiner*, 25 June 1893, p. 17.

42. "The Lights Of London," *Examiner*, 31 December 1893, p. 18.

43. "William Nye Invests In A Brand-New Comet."

44. "All About A Genuine Poet," *World*, 17 June 1888, p. 17.

45. "Bill Nye's Hen Tracks," *Examiner*, 5 June 1892, p. 17.

46. "A Good Night's Sleep," *Examiner*, 19 June 1892, p. 18; "Bill Nye By Special Wire," *Examiner*, 8 July 1894, p. 13.

47. "Hard Work To Stay On Pegasus," *Examiner*, 16 December 1894, p. 18.

48. See "William Visits Eugene," *Examiner*, 28 February 1892, p. 17; "Bill Nye And Royalty," *World*, 18 August 1889, p. 9; "Bill Nye Visits Atlanta," *World*, 23 December 1888, p. 13; "People Nye Has Met," *World*, 22 June 1890, p. 28.

49. "How They Nail Thoughts," *World*, 16 June 1889, p. 21.

50. "The Lights Of London."

51. "Browning Is Not The Man," *World*, 11 November 1888, p. 17.

52. "Just Off Piccadilly," *Examiner*, 5 November 1893, p. 17.

53. "Bill And Bichloride," *Examiner*, 7 February 1892, p. 20.

54. "Bill Nye Down In Pa.," *World*, 8 February 1891, p. 11.
55. "Bill Nye By Special Wire," *Examiner*, 8 July 1894, p. 13.
56. "Jay Gould And Tolstoi," *World*, 12 October 1890, p. 26.
57. *Bill Nye's Thinks* (Chicago: Dearborn Publishing, 1888); hereafter cited in the text as *T*.
58. "New Books And New Editions," *The Book Buyer*, 3d ser. (February 1889), 29.
59. "Minor Notices," *The Critic*, 11 (26 January 1889), 42.
60. *An Almanac For 1891* (New York: Edgar Wilson Nye, [1890]); hereafter cited in the text as *A*.
61. See chapter 6, "Alamancs," in my *Josh Billings* (New York: Twayne, 1973), pp. 92–104.
62. Edgar Wilson Nye, letter to J. B. Pond, 31 August 1890 (Hebard letters).
63. Edgar Wilson Nye, letter to J. B. Pond, 21 September [1890?] (Hebard letters).
64. F. W. Nye, p. 292.
65. Ibid.
66. See Edgar Wilson Nye, letter to J. B. Pond, 20 June [1891?] (Hebard letters).
67. Rush, p. 15 (letter of Nye to Mr. Marshall, 10 Janaury 1892).
68. F. W. Nye, p. 346.

Chapter Six

1. "Nye On Various Themes," *Examiner*, 9 September 1894, p. 18.
2. "Bill Nye Home Again," *Examiner*, 18 October 1891, p. 14.
3. "Rules For Farm Work," *Examiner*, 2 July 1893, p. 18; "A Farmer To The Farmers," *Examiner*, 1 September 1895, p. 18.
4. "Truck Seeds In Politics," *Examiner*, 14 January 1894, p. 15.
5. "Some Idle Thoughts," *Examiner*, 6 March 1892, p. 25.
6. "Farm Philosophy," *Examiner*, 4 September 1892, p. 6.
7. "It Is Bearly Possible," *Examiner*, 18 September 1892, p. 17.
8. "Bill Nye, Ornithologist," *Examiner*, 29 July 1894, p. 15; "Prof. B. Nye on the Bird," *Examiner*, 6 August 1894, p. 24.
9. "Mr. Nye on the Oyster," *Examiner*, 17 November 1895, p. 24.
10. "Various Kinds of Dogs," *Examiner*, 29 January 1893, p. 18.
11. "Enjoying the Exhibits," *Examiner*, 1 October 1893, p. 13.
12. "Garner's Monkey Lore," *Examiner*, 4 February 1894, p. 24.
13. "Both Progress And Poverty," *Examiner*, 23 September 1894, p. 18.
14. Prescott, p. 5.
15. "William Nye Wrestles With Cow Poets," *Examiner*, 22 December 1895, p. 24.

16. "Bill Nye on the Crops," *Examiner*, 6 September 1891, p. 14; "Prof. B. Nye on the Bird."

17. "Bill Nye's Home Life," *Examiner*, 20 September 1891, p. 16.

18. "Bill Nye As A Boomer," *Examiner*, 29 May 1892, p. 15.

19. Ibid.

20. "Slang in Restaurants," *Examiner*, 11 December 1892, p. 14.

21. "Back to Cedric's Days," *Examiner*, 23 July 1893, p. 14.

22. "Ward M'Nye's Notes," *Examiner*, 27 September 1891, p. 14.

23. "Some Gladsome Gayety," *Examiner*, 7 August 1892, p. 17.

24. Ibid.

25. "Nye Treats of Widowers," *Examiner*, 2 June 1895, p. 15.

26. Even in his series of interesting articles on the Chicago World's Fair of 1893, Nye tends to dwell on personalities and human interest stories rather than the proceedings of the fair. He addresses most of his fair "letters" to son Henry, and the son becomes the focus of the writing, Nye offering Chesterfieldian advice while shaping his observations of the fair for his son. He tells Henry the papers are so full of news of the fair that it would be repetitious to recap the goings-on in these letters ("Nye's Deal In Stocks," *Examiner*, 24 September 1893, p. 13). Thus, the fair provides Nye with little more than a framework for his writings. His accounts of the spectacle contrast markedly with Henry Blake Fuller's preoccupation with the Chicago fair and its meaning for the 1890s and the future.

27. "Among The H'Upper Ten," *Examiner*, 26 November 1893, p. 14.

28. "Two Sad, Sad Stories," *Examiner*, 24 December 1893, p. 21.

29. F. W. Nye, p. 348.

30. "William Nye, Lackney," *Examiner*, 19 November 1893, p. 13.

31. F. W. Nye, p. 370.

32. Ibid., p. 374.

33. "Some Chunks of Horse Sense," *Examiner*, 7 April 1895, p. 22.

34. "The Silver Tongued," *Examiner*, 13 January 1895, p. 18.

35. "He Wore An 'Examiner,'" *Examiner*, 10 February 1895, p. 19; "Nye Makes His Social Debut," *Examiner*, 17 February 1895, p. 18.

36. "He Wore An 'Examiner.'"

37. Ibid.

38. "Some Chunks of Horse Sense"; also see "Information At Cost Price," *Examiner*, 9 June 1895, p. 21.

39. "Bill Nye On Royalty And Things," *Examiner*, 3 March 1895, p. 18; also "Bill Nye's Birds-Eye View of the U.S. Senate," *Examiner*, 27 Janaury 1895, p. 19.

40. "Bill Nye On Government," *Examiner*, 24 February 1895, p. 18.

41. Ibid.

42. "William Nye's Ideas of the Monroe Doctrine," *Examiner*, 29 December 1895, p. 24.

43. "Some Chunks of Horse Sense," and "Information At Cost Price."

44. "Bill Nye on the Corrugated Sea," *Examiner*, 10 March 1895, p. 18.

45. The "third" play and the one whose authorship is in serious doubt is *Stung*, a three-act comedy entered for copyright in 1912, sixteen years after Nye's death. The only extant copy, a typescript in the U.S. Copyright Office, bears the name Edgar Wilson Nye as author. Despite the fact that the play has some resemblance to Nye's other works in tone and subject, it is of doubtful Nye authorship because (1) of the lapse in time between his death in 1896 and the year of copyright, and (2) the textual references to titles of popular novels and magazines that were not yet in circulation during Nye's lifetime. Of course, the play could have been touched up and "modernized" by a family member or literary executor, but such a move seems highly unlikely since the play was not in public demand and likely was never performed. Therefore, it must be the work of a later Edgar Wilson Nye. (The Library of Congress has attempted to find out more about the registration for copyright, but has been unable to produce further information about the author or circumstances of the copyright application.)

46. "Mr. Nye Sees Henry Irving," *Examiner*, 24 November 1895, p. 32.

47. "Bill Nye's Sunday Off," *World*, 22 September 1889, p. 21; "Bill Nye Goes Visiting," *Examiner*, 23 August 1891, p. 13.

48. "Bill Nye Goes Visiting," *Examiner*, 23 August 1891, p. 13.

49. "William Nye's Ideas of the Monroe Doctrine."

50. See, for example, "Bill Nye At the Ballet," *World*, 18 January 1891, p. 22, and "An Operatic Entertainment," *R*, pp. 154–56.

51. "Nye In San Francisco," *Examiner*, 2 April 1893, p. 14.

52. "Elevation of the Stage," *Examiner*, 26 August 1894, p. 19; "Uncle Tom's Cabin," *FL*, pp. 282–85.

53. "Bill Nye and J. Caesar," *World*, 1 January 1888, p. 9; reprinted in *RG* as "Julius Caesar In Town," pp. 17–22.

54. "Bill Nye As A High Critic," *World*, 22 April 1888, p. 17; reprinted in *Ludlow* as "A Singular 'Hamlet,'" pp. 81–91.

55. "Hamlet on the Half Shell," *Examiner*, 26 May 1895, p. 24.

56. The exception, of course, is *Stung* (see note 45). The author has conducted an extensive search for Nye's plays in leading libraries and drama collections throughout the world. It appears that no copies survive, unless they reside somewhere in obscurity, perhaps unknown to their owner.

57. According to *Dramatic Compositions Copyrighted in the United States—1870–1916* (Washington: Library of Congress—U.S. Copyright Office, 1918), I, 779, no. 15927.

58. F. W. Nye, p. 150.

59. For background of *The Cadi* see Paul L. Armstrong, "History of the Post Office at Laramie, Wyoming," *Annals of Wyoming*, 11 (January 1939), 52–60; also F. W. Nye, pp. 305–8.

60. The play is listed in *Dramatic Compositions Copyrighted in the United States* (I, 271, no. 5793) as being published by Francis, Valentine, & Co. of San Francisco in 1891. No copy has turned up, however.

61. For example, see "Bill Nye's 'Cadi,'" *The Critic*, 16 (26 September 1891), p. 157.

62. "The Prodigal Son" is located in the Houghton Library at Harvard University. Jacob Blanck lists it as being copyrighted in 1891 by Hitchcock & McCargo Publishing Co. (Limited), New York, 1891 (*Bibliography of American Literature*, vol. 6 [New Haven: Yale University Press, 1973], p. 475).

63. "The Cadi," *New York Times*, 22 September 1891, p. 4.

64. "The Week at the Theatres," *World*, 13 December 1891, p. 16.

65. "The Week at the Theatres," *World*, 20 December 1891, p. 14.

66. See, for example, "The Week at the Theatres," *World*, 8 November 1891, p. 16.

67. "The Week at the Theatres," *World*, 6 December 1891, p. 16.

68. For some unknown reason, *The Stag Party* was never copyrighted.

69. "The Theatres," *New York Times*, 15 December 1895, p. 12.

70. According to *New York Times* review, "A New Musical Travesty," 18 December 1895, p. 4.

71. Ibid.

72. "The Theatres," *New York Times*, 22 December 1895, p. 12.

73. Ibid.

74. "A New Musical Travesty," *New York Times*, 18 December 1895, p. 4.

75. "Merry Christmas to Players and Playgoers," *World*, 15 December 1895, p. 26.

76. "It Proved A Very Flat Stag Party," *World*, 18 December 1895, p. 9.

77. Ibid.

78. F. W. Nye, p. 398.

79. Ibid.

80. Blair, "The Background of Bill Nye," p. 60.

81. "Going to Jerusalem," *Examiner*, 6 January 1895, p. 19; "Nye and the Puritans," *Examiner*, 16 August 1891, p. 13.

82. Blair, "The Background of Bill Nye," p. 60.

83. *Bill Nye's History of the United States* (Philadelphia: Lippincott, 1894), p. 6; hereafter cited in the text as *US*.

84. Lippincott, p. 605.

85. Ibid.

86. Blair, "The Background of Bill Nye," p. 127; Larson, "Laramie's Bill Nye," p. 47.

87. Edgar Wilson Nye, letter to J. B. Pond, 7 June 1894 (Hebard letters).

88. Actually, something of a "germ" for the comic history of England appears in "William Nye, Cockney," *Examiner*, 19 November 1893, p. 13.

89. Lippincott, p. 605.

90. *Bill Nye's History of England from The Druids to the Reign of Henry VIII* (Philadelphia: Lippincott, 1896), p. 5; hereafter cited in the text as *E*.

156   BILL NYE

91. Nye was responsible for chap. 12. pp. 169–87. Other writers involved
in *His Fleeting Ideal*, as listed on the title page, were P. T. Barnum, John L.
Sullivan, Ella Wheeler Wilcox, Alfred C. Calhoun, Howe & Hummel, Inspec-
tor Byrnes, Pauline Hall, Miss Eastlake, W. H. Ballou, Nell Nelson, and Alan
Dale.

92. It is curious that nowhere in the four newspaper columns on his Bahamas excursion does Nye refer to his manuscript or its loss, though he does say
in a letter to his wife that he recovered almost all his belongings except that
book (F. W. Nye, p. 375).

93. *A Guest at the Ludlow* (Indianapolis: Bowen-Merrill, 1897); hereafter
cited in the text as *L*. The last essay in the book is not by Nye: on James
Whitcomb Riley's poetry by one "Chelifer," the essay is reprinted from
Godey's Magazine and was apparently included by the publishers as a pro-
motional piece, since a price list of Riley's works follows the essay.

94. Eitel, p. 484.

95. "Bill Nye's Last Book," *Overland Monthly*, 29 (March 1897), 336.

96. Such as the piece "Earning A Reward," pp. 156–61, which is a rewritten, longer version of "The Opium Habit" appearing in *R*, pp. 63–64.

97. Davidson, p. 17.

98. The date of *Bill Nye's Grim Jokes* is undetermined. Jacob Blanck
states it is not earlier than 1890 (VI, 478).

99. Blanck says both *Boomerang Shots* and *Hits and Skits* were published
in 1884 (VI, 470–71).

100. As Blanck has already pointed out (VI, 471).

101. *The Funny Fellows Grab-Bag. By Bill Nye and Other Funny Men*
(New York: Ogilvie, 1903). The copies I examined are in the Houghton
Library at Harvard and the University of North Carolina Library at Chapel
Hill.

Chapter Seven

1. Walter Blair, *Horse Sense in American Humor* (Chicago: University
of Chicago Press, 1942), p. 180.

2. Ibid., pp. 180, 185.

3. Walter Blair, *Native American Humor* (San Francisco: Chandler,
1960), p. 105.

4. Blair, *Horse Sense*, pp. 180, 182.

5. Twain's jealousy of Nye is a point made by Walter McDougall in "Pictures in the Papers," *The American Mercury*, 6 (September 1925), 73.

6. *The Autobiography of Mark Twain*, ed. Charles Neider (New York:
Harper and Brothers, 1959), p. 223.

7. Julian Hawthorne and Leonard Lemmon, *American Literature* (Boston: D. C. Heath, 1901), p. 318.

8. Clemens, *Famous Funny Fellows*, p. 117.

9. "Bill Nye's Entertainment," *Colorado Springs Gazette*, 5 March 1890.

10. "Nye And Burbank," *Denver Republican*, 10 February 1893.

11. "The Lounger," *The Critic*, 11 (15 June 1889), p. 297.

12. "Bill Nye's Entertainment."

13. Lippincott, p. 605.

14. Eitel, p. 479.

15. "Bill Nye Is Dead," *World*, 23 February 1896, p. 7.

16. "Poet Riley's Testimonial," ibid.

17. "Bill Nye's Life Is At An End," *Examiner*, 23 February 1896, p. 1.

18. "Edgar W. Nye, The Man Without An Enemy," *Examiner*, 23 February 1896, p. 6.

19. "Humorist Nye Is Dead," *New York Times*, 23 February 1896, p. 11.

20. Denham Sutcliffe, ed. *Untriangulated Stars: Letters of Edwin Arlington Robinson to Harry De Forest Smith 1890–1905* (Cambridge, Mass.: Harvard University Press, 1947), p. 43.

21. Ibid.

22. Mark Twain, *Autobiography*, p. 272.

23. Ibid, p. 273.

24. O. N. Gibson, "Bill Nye," *Annals of Wyoming*, 3 (July 1925), 101.

25. William Dean Howells, ["Our National Humorists"]. "Editors Easy Chair," *Harpers*, 134 (February 1917), 442.

26. William W. Ellsworth, *A Golden Age of Authors* (Boston: Houghton Mifflin, 1919), p. 218.

27. Hancock, p. 602.

28. Ibid., p. 603.

29. Eitel, p. 474.

30. James L. Ford, "A Century Of American Humor," *Munsey's Magazine*, 25 (July 1901), 487–88.

31. Ibid., p. 488.

32. Ibid.

33. Chaplin, "Bill Nye," pp. 223, 224.

34. Ibid., p. 223.

35. Chaplin, "Bill Nye In Laramie," pp. 142–43.

36. Debs, p. 10.

37. Ibid., p. 11.

38. William Lightfoot Visscher, *Ten Wise Men and Some More* (Chicago: Atwell, 1909), p. 96.

39. Ibid., p. 97.

40. Leacock, "American Humor," p. 452.

41. Stephen Leacock, *The Greatest Pages of American Humor* (Garden City: Doubleday, Doran, 1936), p. 155.

42. George Frisbie Whicher, "Minor Humorists," in *Cambridge History of American Literature* (New York: Macmillan, 1931), III, 27.

43. Leacock, "Edgar Wilson Nye," pp. 599–600.

44. Ibid., p. 600.

45. Douglas C. McMurtrie, "Pioneer Printing In Wyoming," *Annals of Wyoming*, 9 (January 1933), 739.

46. T. A. Larson, *Bill Nye's Western Humor* (Lincoln: University of Nebraska Press, 1968).

47. Ibid., p. xiii.

48. Such as Diane Heestand's "The Writing of Bill Nye in Laramie" (see chapter 2, note 30).

49. Such as the syndicated article on Nye by United Press writer Dan Chiszar (see preface, note 1).

50. Van Wyck Brooks, *The Confident Years: 1885–1915* (New York: E. P. Dutton, 1952), p. 69.

51. Jesse Bier, *The Rise and Fall of American Humor* (Chicago: Holt, Rinehart & Winston, 1968), pp. 78, 87, 109, 190.

52. C. Carroll Hollis, "Rural Humor of the Late Nineteenth Century," in *The Comic Imagination in American Literature*, ed. Louis D. Rubin, Jr. (New Brunswick: Rutgers University Press, 1973), p. 169.

53. Jay Martin, "Ambrose Bierce," in *The Comic Imagination in American Literature*, p. 199.

54. Walter Blair and Hamlin Hill, *America's Humor from Poor Richard to Doonesbury* (New York: Oxford University Press, 1978), pp. 289–90.

55. G. D. Eaton, "When Bill Nye's Humor Was Funny," *The Literary Digest International Book Review*, 4, no. 12 (November 1926), 769.

56. Larson, "Laramie's Bill Nye," p. 54.

57. Hollis, p. 175.

58. Bier, p. 116.

59. "Nye, Edgar Wilson," *The New Encyclopaedia Britannica* (Chicago: Encyclopaedia Britannica, Inc., 1979), micropaedia, VII, 452.

60. Larson, *Bill Nye's Western Humor*, p. xiii.

Selected Bibliography

PRIMARY SOURCES

Listed below are the most significant books by Bill Nye, collections of his letters, and anthologies of his works. This listing of primary materials does not include Nye's several hundred newspaper and magazine contributions, of course, or reprints of his articles in pamphlet form. Nor does it include the many reprintings of his books under different titles. The most complete primary bibliographies, which supplement my listing, are those by Jacob Blanck, *Bibliography of American Literature*, vol. 6 (New Haven: Yale University Press, 1973), pp. 468–82 (a descriptive bibliography); Walter Blair, "The Background of Bill Nye in American Humor" (Ph.D. diss., University of Chicago, 1931), pp. 129–31; and Lloyd McFarling, "Bibliography and Works of *Bill Nye*," a typescript (n.d.) which resides in the Hebard Room of the University of Wyoming library. All three of these bibliographies list Nye's reprinted books under their various titles (which sometimes changed with every republication).

The most exhaustive repository of works, letters, and documents both by and on Bill Nye is in the Bill Nye Collection of the American Heritage Center, University of Wyoming library. Numerous letters and manuscripts, however, are in libraries throughout the United States (see J. Albert Robbins, ed., *American Literary Manuscripts*, 2d ed. [Athens: University of Georgia Press, 1977], p. 237).

1. Major Books

Baled Hay: A Drier Book Than Walt Whitman's "Leaves o' Grass." Chicago: Belford, Clarke, 1884.

Bill Nye and Boomerang: or, The Tale of a Meek-Eyed Mule, and Some Other Literary Gems. Chicago: Belford, Clarke, 1881.

Bill Nye's Chestnuts Old and New: Latest Gathering. Chicago: Belford, Clarke, 1888.

Bill Nye's History of England from the Druids to the Reign of Henry VIII. Philadelphia: J. B. Lippincott, 1896.

Bill Nye's History of the United States. Philadelphia: J. B. Lippincott, 1894.

Bill Nye's Thinks. Chicago: Dearborn Publishing, 1888.

Forty Liars, and Other Lies. Chicago: Belford, Clarke, 1882.

A Guest at the Ludlow and Other Stories. Indianapolis: Bowen-Merrill, 1897.

Nye and Riley's Railway Guide. Chicago: Dearborn Publishing, 1888. Written with James Whitcomb Riley.
Remarks. Chicago: A. E. Davis, 1887.

2. Other Books
An Almanac for 1891 by Bill Nye. New York: Edgar Wilson Nye, 1890.
Bill Nye's Blossom Rock. Chicago?, 1885. Probably pirated.
Bill Nye's Cordwood. Chicago: Rhodes & McClure Publishing, 1887. Probably pirated.
Bill Nye's Grim Jokes. Chicago: W. B. Conkey, n.d. Jacob Blanck says not published before 1890.
Boomerang Shots. London and New York: Ward, Lock, n.d. (ca. 1884).
The Funny Fellow's Grab-Bag. By Bill Nye and Other Funny Men. New York: J. S. Ogilvie, 1903. Contributions by Nye and several anonymous humorous writers.
His Fleeting Ideal: A Romance of Baffled Hypnotism. New York: J. S. Ogilvie, 1890. A composite novel for which Nye wrote chapter 12.
Hits and Skits. London: Ward, Lock, n.d. (ca. 1884).
Nye and Riley's Wit and Humor. Amusing Prose Sketches and Quaint Dialect Poems. Chicago: W. B. Conkey, 1901. Not a reprint of *Railway Guide.*

3. Published Letters
EITEL, EDMUND H., ed. "Letters of Riley and Bill Nye." *Harper's Magazine*, 138 (March 1919), 474–84.
NYE, FRANK WILSON. *Bill Nye: His Own Life Story.* New York: Century Co., 1926.
RUSH, NIXON ORWIN, ed. *Letters of Edgar Wilson Nye Now in the University of Wyoming Library.* Laramie: University of Wyoming Library, 1950.

4. Anthologies
GUNN, JOHN W., ed. *The Humor of "Bill" Nye.* Girard, Kansas: Haldeman-Julius, 1924.
HASLEY, LOUIS, ed. *The Best of Bill Nye's Humor.* New Haven: College and University Press, 1972.
LARSON, T. A., ed. *Bill Nye's Western Humor.* Lincoln: University of Nebraska Press, 1968. Contains a bibliography, pp. xv–xvi.

SECONDARY SOURCES

1. Bibliography
Besides the University of Wyoming library, the most extensive collections of materials about Bill Nye are found in the Albany County Library in Laramie,

Wyoming, the University of North Carolina library (Chapel Hill), the Pack Memorial Library in Asheville, N.C., the Bancroft Library of the University of California at Berkeley, and the State Historical Society of Wisconsin. Published and unpublished checklists of works on Nye are included in books and articles by Lloyd McFarling and T. A. Larson (cited above); and by Diane E. Heestand, David B. Kesterson, and Ethel Leona Lindsey (cited below).

2. Biography and Criticism
ARMSTRONG, PAUL L. "History of the Post Office at Laramie, Wyoming." *Annals of Wyoming*, 11 (January 1939), 52–60. A brief account of Nye's life in Laramie, especially his newspaper work and postmastership. Includes snippets from Nye's works about post office service and customers.
BIER, JESSE. *The Rise and Fall of American Humor*. New York: Holt, Rinehart & Winston, 1968. Deals with Nye as a representative of his school in techniques and realistic criticism. Mentions his influence on Finley Peter Dunne.
"Bill Nye and Whitcomb Riley." *New York World*, 25 November 1888, p. 16. Discusses the humorous manner of each comedian and the earnings of Nye as columnist and lecturer.
"Bill Nye at His Home." *New York World*, 8 February 1891, p. 11. An interview with and feature on the Nye family at Tompkinsville, Staten Island.
BLAIR, WALTER. "The Background of Bill Nye in American Humor." Ph.D. dissertation, University of Chicago, 1931. The pilot twentieth-century study of Nye's humor. Relates Nye to earlier American humor, outlines types of humor he used, and discusses his humorous traits.
———. "Burlesques in Nineteenth-Century American Humor." *American Literature*, 2 (November 1930), 236–47. Discusses Nye's burlesques of oratory and fiction, especially the latter.
———. *Horse Sense in American Humor*. Chicago: University of Chicago Press, 1942. Nye as the last of the nineteenth-century school of humorists; how he played dual role of fool and horse-sense philosopher.
———. *Native American Humor*. San Francisco: Chandler Publishing, 1960. Originally published in 1937 as *Native American Humor (1800–1900)*, the book contains many references to Nye's humorous traits and reprints three selections by Nye.
———. "The Popularity of Nineteenth-Century American Humorists." *American Literature*, 3 (May 1931), 175–94. A fairly detailed survey of Nye's career, popularity, and successes.
BRYANT, BYRON. *Humor in the 19th Century*. Los Angeles: Pacifica Tape Library, [196?]. A sound recording on Josh Billings, Artemus Ward, Bill Nye. Bryant discusses the three writers as independent, irreverent American humorists and reads from their works. Says Nye is especially good at ridiculing high-flown American Romantic writers.

BURRAGE, FRANK SUMNER. "Bill Nye (1850–1896)." *Annals of Wyoming*, 18 (January 1946), 79–87. Biographical survey of Nye's life, especially good on the Western years.

CHAPLIN, W. E. "Bill Nye." *The Frontier*, 11 (March 1931), 223–26. A brief sketch of Nye's personality and his newspaper career in Laramie by a fellow journalist.

————. "Bill Nye in Laramie." In *Second Biennial Report, State Historian of Wyoming*. Sheridan, Wy.: Mills Co., 1921–1923. Pp. 142–58. An extremely valuable, detailed contemporary glimpse of Nye's life and career in Laramie

————. "Some of the Early Newspapers of Wyoming." *Wyoming Historical Society Miscellanies 1919*. Laramie: Laramie Republican Co., 1919. Pp. 7–24. A helpful catalog of the early Wyoming newspapers with which Nye was associated. Details Nye's involvement with each and gives their histories.

————. "Some Wyoming Editors I Have Known." *Annals of Wyoming*, 18 (January 1946), 79–87. Largely a rehash of the earlier articles with emphasis on Chaplin's personal relationship with each editor (including Nye).

CHISZAR, DAN. ["Bill Nye: Forgotten Humorist"]. United Press International syndicated column, November–December 1978. A retrospective view of the now relatively unknown humorist. Reviews his life and samples a few of Nye's humorous quips.

CLARKE, MABELL SHIPPIE. "Edgar Wilson Nye." *The Writer*, 9 (March 1896), 34–35. A local writer discusses Nye's writings from Arden, N.C., near Asheville.

CLEMENS, WILL M. *Famous Funny Fellows: Brief Biographical Sketches of American Humorists*. Cleveland: William W. Williams, 1882. Important as a contemporaneous account of Nye and his newspaper writings in Laramie. Clemens attests to Nye's great popularity and gives examples of his humor.

DAVIDSON, LEVETTE J. "'Bill' Nye and The Denver Tribune." *The Colorado Magazine*, 4 (January 1927), 13–18. An important look at Nye's work for and relationship with the *Tribune*. Also examines comic techniques and satirical targets.

DEBS, EUGENE V. *Riley, Nye & Field: Personal Notes and Recollections*. N.p., n.d. A pamphlet in which Debs recounts his friendship with Nye. Briefly discusses Nye's humor and satire.

DICKEY, MARCUS. *The Maturity of James Whitcomb Riley*. Indianapolis: Bobbs-Merrill, 1922. Many references to Nye, but especially important is chapter 13, "The Unique Combination," which treats Nye and Riley together on the lecture circuit.

EATON, G. D. "When Bill Nye's Humor Was Funny." *The Literary Digest International Book Review*, 4, no. 12 (November 1926), 769, 779. An essay-review on Frank Wilson Nye's *Bill Nye: His Own Life Story*, but comments on Nye's humor and his failure to survive because of changing public tastes.

EDWARDS, E. J. "Nye, the Humorist." *Colorado Springs Daily Gazette*, 17 January 1892, p. [8]. Concerns Nye's start and rise to fame on the *Laramie Boomerang*. A syndicated article by the American Press Association.

FORD, JAMES L. "A Century of American Humor." *Munsey's Magazine*, 25 (July 1901), 482–90. A short but important appraisal of Nye, seeing him as succeeding Mark Twain as leader of the literary comedians.

FORD, ROBERT. *American Humourists*. London: Alexander Gardner, 1897. The chapter "Bill Nye" gives a Briton's view of Nye's poetry, prose, and humorous techniques. Also gives biographical sketch.

GIBSON, O. N. "Bill Nye." *Annals of Wyoming*, 3 (July 1925), 95–104. An address given on Nye in Riverton, Wyoming, stressing biographical facts and critical appraisal of Nye's humor.

HANCOCK, ALBERT E. "Bill Nye and His Work." In "Bill Nye—The Inimitable: His Work and His Personality." *Book Lovers Magazine*, 1 (June 1903), 591–605. A general account of Nye's life and a good, helpful analysis of his humor.

HEESTAND, DIANE ELISSA. "The Writing of Bill Nye in Laramie." M.A. thesis, University of Wyoming, 1968. Valuable in that it makes use of a number of unpublished source materials in exploring Nye's life and career in the West. A bibliography appears on pp. 49–56.

HOLLIS, C. CARROLL. "Rural Humor of the Late Nineteenth Century." In *The Comic Imagination in American Literature*, edited by Louis D. Rubin, Jr. Brunswick: Rutgers University Press, 1973. Treats Nye as a talented and perceptive writer who transcended role of newspaper humorist because of his popularity. Mixed appraisal. Feels Nye's books unreadable by modern audience due to brevity and similarity in format of his collected columns.

KESTERSON, DAVID B. *Bill Nye: The Western Writings*. Western Writers Series. Boise, Idaho: Boise State University, 1976. A monograph on Nye's writing while he lived in Laramie. Studies the influence of the West on his development as a humorist. A bibliography appears on pp. 45–48.

LANDON, MELVILLE D. *Kings of the Platform and Pulpit*. Chicago: Werner, 1895. Chapter on Nye gives brief biography and Landon's reminiscences of Nye. Very important on Nye as lecturer; gives an example of his presentation.

LARSON, T. A. *History of Wyoming*. Lincoln: University of Nebraska Press, 1965. Several passages treat Nye's life in the West and his favorite subjects.

———. "Laramie's Bill Nye." In *The Denver West—1952 Brand Book*. Denver: The Westerners, 1953. Pp. 34–56. An excellent, informative article about Nye in Laramie: his journalism, his books, his local associations.

LEACOCK, STEPHEN. "Edgar Wilson Nye." In *Dictionary of American Biog-*

raphy, edited by Dumas Malone, XIII, 598–600. New York: Charles Scribner's Sons, 1934. Undoubtedly the best encyclopedia-length article on Nye: thorough and accurate in facts and perceptive in evaluation. Extremely helpful.

―――. *The Greatest Pages of American Humor*. Garden City: Doubleday, Doran, 1936. Briefly treats Nye in the role of "self-confessed idiot" and as the "after-Mark" of American Humor.

LINDSEY, ETHEL LEONA. "Edgar Wilson Nye and American Humor." M.A. thesis, University of Wyoming, 1929. Discusses influence of Nye's background on his humor and formally analyzes his humor. Valuable in that Lindsey interviewed people who actually knew Nye. A bibliography appears on pp. 89–96.

LIPPINCOTT, J. B. "Bill Nye as Viewed by His Publisher." In "Bill Nye—The Inimitable: His Work and His Personality." *Book Lovers Magazine*, 1 (June 1903), 605. The publisher of Nye's two comic histories discusses the comedian's character and literary traits. A brief but important view.

[McDOUGALL, WALTER]. "Bill Nye as Seen by Walt McDougall." In "Bill Nye—The Inimitable: His Work and His Personality." *Book Lovers Magazine*, 1 (June 1903), 604–5. An interesting personal glimpse of Nye by the cartoonist who illustrated Nye's columns for the New York *World*.

―――. "Pictures in the Papers." *American Mercury*, 6 (September 1925), 67–73. Especially interesting in its discussion of the Nye-Twain relationship, emphasizing Twain's jealousy of Nye.

MEAD, LEON. "Eugene Field and Bill Nye: A Reminiscence and an Original Manuscript." *The Bookman*, 9 (April 1899), 135–36. An account of the author's meeting Nye in the West and Nye's presenting him with a manuscript poem about the death of his son.

MURRELL, WILLIAM. *A History of American Graphic Humor*. Vol. 2, (1865–1938). New York: Macmillan, 1938. Refers to Nye's works in conjunction with their illustrators.

NYE, FRANK WILSON. *Bill Nye: His Own Life Story*. New York: Century, 1926. The single most important work on Nye for biography. Here Nye's son allows his father to tell most of his own story through letters, the result being a sort of biography-autobiography.

PHELPS, WILLIAM LYON, ed. *Letters of James Whitcomb Riley*. Indianapolis: Bobbs-Merrill, 1930. Many references to Nye, and letters from Riley to Nye.

POND, J. B. *Eccentricities of Genius*. New York: G. W. Dillingham, 1900. A brief chapter of personal reminiscences by Nye's lecture manager.

PRESCOTT, AUGUSTA. "The Family of a Humorist." *The Ladies Home Journal*, 12 (March 1895), 5. An article on the Nyes at home in Arden, N.C. Interesting view of their family life and a good portrait of Fanny Nye, Nye's wife.

REVELL, PETER. *James Whitcomb Riley*. New York: Twayne Publishers, 1970. Passim on the Nye-Riley relationship.

SEARIGHT, FRANK THOMPSON, ed. *The American Press Humorists' Book*. "Bill" Nye Monument Edition. Los Angeles: Frank Thompson Searight, 1907. The Nye portion mainly consists of a series of articles on and tributes to him written by members of the press. Helpful personal and critical remarks on Nye. Good photographs of Nye and places associated with him.

SEITZ, DON C. "The Last of the Old School." *The Literary Review*, 7, No. 8 (16 October 1926), p. 1. An essay-review of F. W. Nye's *Bill Nye: His Own Life Story*. Reassesses Nye's humor and reviews his life in some detail.

SPRAGUE, JOHN FRANCIS. "Edgar Wilson Nye." In *Collections of the Piscataquis County Historical Society*. Dover, Maine: Observer Press, 1910. I, 147–53. A brief account of Nye's life and works, emphasizing his Maine birth and ties.

VISSCHER, WILLIAM LIGHTFOOT. *Ten Wise Men and Some More*. Chicago: Atwell Printing and Binding, 1909. A personal remembrance of Nye with biographical facts and Visscher's impressions of his personality and humor.

WILDER, MARSHALL P. *The Sunny Side of the Street*. New York: Funk and Wagnalls, 1905. A fairly superficial, though personal, remembrance of Nye. Mainly an account of Nye's genial nature and his popularity. Some glaring factual errors.

Index